This book has been donated to the
Thomas Crane Public Library
by the

Rotary Club of Quincy

in honor of:

CAROL M. FLYNN
Quincy Police Department
H.E.L.P. Program
Project Lifesaver

Guest speaker: June 11, 2013

WORLD WAR II

THE HOME FRONTS

ALLIED AND AXIS LIFE DURING WORLD WAR II

Peter Darman, Editor

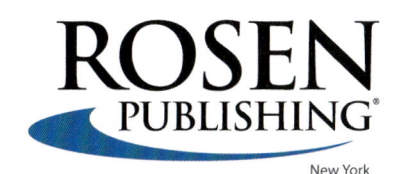

Rosen PUBLISHING

New York

This edition is published in 2013 by:

The Rosen Publishing Group, Inc.
29 East 21st Street, New York, NY 10010

Copyright © 2013 Brown Bear Books Ltd.

All rights reserved. No part of this book may be reproduced in any form without permission in writing from the publisher, except by a reviewer.

For Brown Bear Books Ltd:
Editorial Director: Lindsey Lowe
Senior Editor: Tim Cooke
Military Editor: Pete Darman
Children's Publisher: Anne O'Daly
Art Director: Jeni Child
Picture Manager: Sophie Mortimer

Library of Congress Cataloging-in-Publication Data

The home fronts: Allied and Axis life during World War II/editor, Peter Darman.
    p. cm.—(World War II)
Includes bibliographical references and index.
ISBN 978-1-4488-9236-5 (library binding)
1. World War, 1939–1945—Social aspects—Juvenile literature. I. Darman, Peter.
D744.6.H66 2013
940.53—dc23

2012027243

Manufactured in the United States of America

CPSIA Compliance Information: Batch #W13YA: For further information, contact Rosen Publishing, New York, at 1-800-237-9932

Picture Credits:
Front Cover: Robert Hunt Library
All photographs The Robert Hunt Library except:
AKG Images: 42/43; Corbis: Bettmann 11br, 47b; Getty Images: 37, 39; Time & Life Pictures: 52b; Lebrecht Collection: 46; Rue des Archives: 36 tl; Library of Congress: 11tr, 15br, 25tr, 36bc, 40; National Archives: 14; Nik Cornish: 25br; TopFoto: 15tr, 27, 38bl, 45, 52tl; AP Photos: 41; Picturepoint: 28/29
Key: t = top, b = bottom, c = center, l = left, r = right
All Artworks © Brown Bear Books Ltd.

CONTENTS

Chapter 1 — 4
The U.S. home front
Although the U.S. mainland was never attacked by the Japanese, American civilians lived under constant fear of enemy attack and faced rationing. On the other hand, the war boosted the economy and led to greater gender and racial equality as women and ethnic minorities entered the workplace in large numbers.

Chapter 2 — 16
Allied home front: Britain and the Soviet Union
The British people endured rationing, the Blitz, and the threat of invasion during the war, while in the Soviet Union life for civilians was one of unremitting hardship.

Chapter 3 — 28
Axis home fronts
The first three years of the war were relatively peaceful for the populations of the Axis countries, but life then deteriorated rapidly as Allied bombers pounded German and Italian cities, and enemy armies closed in from all directions. In Japan, U.S. submarines stopped any supplies reaching the home islands, and U.S. bombers reduced Japanese cities to ashes.

Chapter 4 — 42
Life in occupied Europe
Life under German occupation was fraught with danger. At any time, civilians could be arrested by the dreaded Gestapo and either shot or shipped off to a concentration camp on the flimsiest of pretexts. Only a small minority collaborated with the hated enemy.

TIMELINE SEPTEMBER 1939–SEPTEMBER 1945 — 56

GLOSSARY — 61

FURTHER READING — 62

INDEX — 63

CHAPTER 1
THE U.S. HOME FRONT

America's entry into the war changed the lives not only of those in the armed forces, but also of those at home. Unlike other countries, though, the United States did not experience the terror of bombing or occupation.

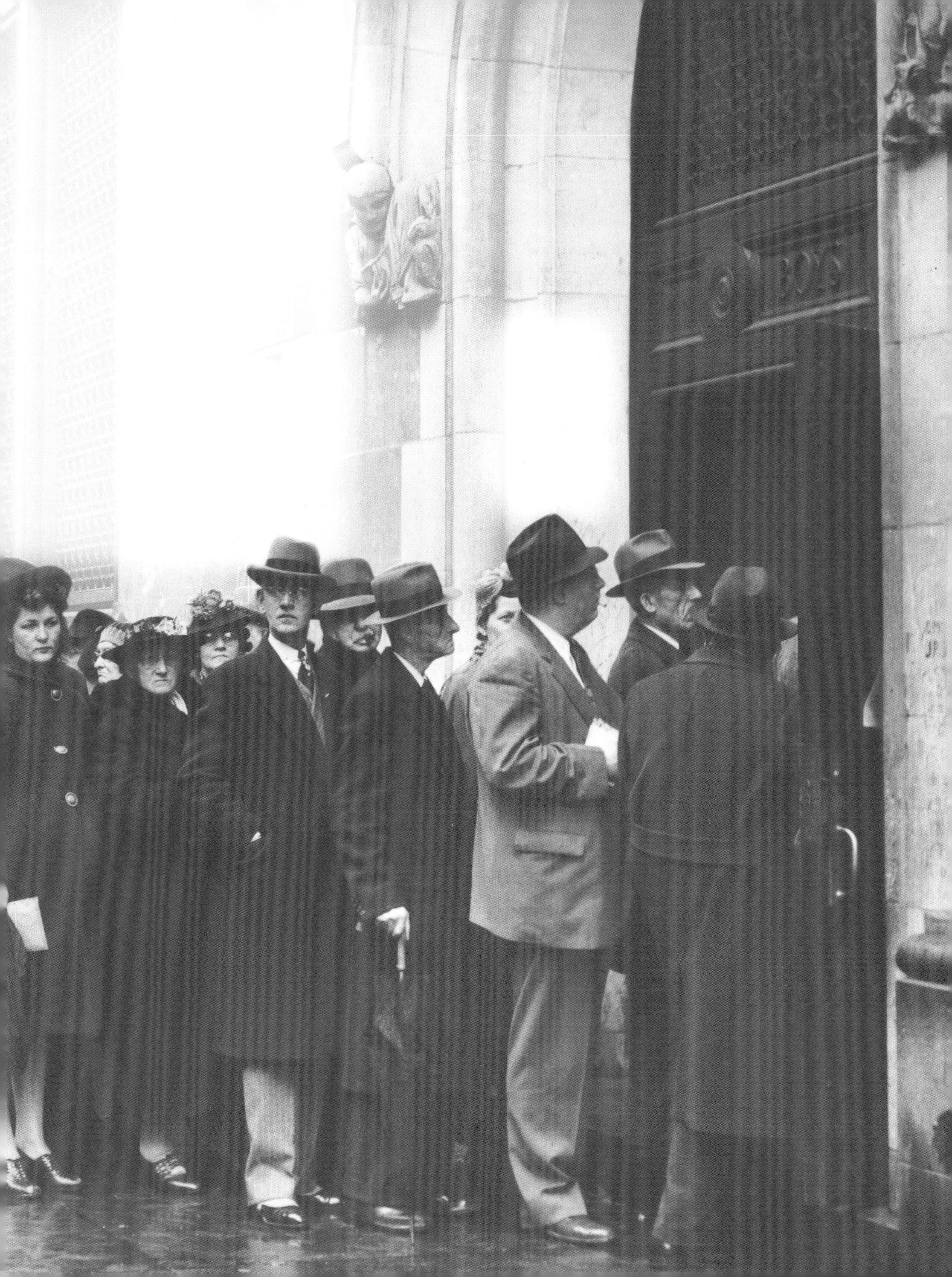

Children wait in line to buy tickets at a movie theater that also sells war bonds. U.S. citizens were encouraged to finance the war effort by loaning their savings to the government.

Previous pages: New York residents line up outside a school to receive their wartime ration books.

The United States was one of the few main combatants to escape military action on its home soil. Hawaii and Alaska, however, which were U.S. territories, were the sites of battles and bombings. The mainland of the United States was largely untouched by conflict. But the country was affected by the war experience in many other ways.

After Pearl Harbor

By December 1941, the conflict in Europe had been raging for over two years. The United States was still at peace, but it was closely involved in the war. President Franklin D. Roosevelt had enabled the nation to provide material and financial aid to the Allies. U.S. shipping had become a target of German U-boats (submarines) in the Atlantic. Technically, however, the United States was still neutral.

That situation changed on December 7, 1941, with the Japanese attack on Pearl Harbor. Roosevelt declared war on Japan the next day. When Germany declared war against the United States on December 11, the nation was fighting on two fronts: against Japan in the Pacific, and against Germany and Italy in Europe.

The Pearl Harbor attack caused widespread panic. Across the country, cities took precautions against enemy air raids, even though they were highly unlikely. Communities along the West Coast worried about enemy troop landings or acts of sabotage.

The onset of war seemed sudden and frightening to many Americans. Their panic and shock, however, were accompanied by rage. They saw the United States as a peaceful nation that had suffered an unprovoked attack. The widespread sense of outrage would fuel the U.S. determination to win the war.

Rationing in the land of plenty

The United States had more wealth and resources than virtually any other power in the war. Many of its citizens enjoyed a higher standard of living than their contemporaries in other countries. The war effort required dramatic changes in the U.S. economy, however. Americans would need to consume less and produce more. Military needs would leave far less oil, steel, rubber, and food for civilians.

To control the distribution of goods, Roosevelt established the Office of Price Administration (OPA). It imposed strict limits on prices and wages to prevent inflation. The OPA also rationed scarce goods: sugar first, followed by meat, butter, and canned goods. Citizens were given ration books that entitled them to buy limited quantities of each item. It was a frustrating experience for shoppers accustomed to full store shelves.

The use of automobiles was severely impacted by the rationing of gasoline.

Eleanor Roosevelt served as a director of the Office for Civilian Defense for less than a year, resigning in protest at budget cuts.

THE FIRST LADY'S BRIEF COMMAND

The Office of Civilian Defense (OCD) was formed in the summer of 1941. It was a response to Germany's bombing campaign against British cities. The government asked New York mayor Fiorello LaGuardia to organize a nationwide system of air-raid warnings and shelters in case of air attack, and a system of blackouts to confuse enemy bombers. LaGuardia asked the first lady, Eleanor Roosevelt, to direct volunteer participation for the OCD. Her job was to coordinate health care, childcare, and physical fitness for civilians serving in the OCD.

Roosevelt soon found herself in political trouble. She appointed as an OCD officer Melvyn Douglas, an actor known for his left-wing beliefs. She also hired a personal friend to develop a dance program for children as part of the OCD physical-fitness program.

Congress responded by symbolically cutting a small part of the OCD's budget. Roosevelt and her appointees resigned in February 1942. Although she no longer held formal office, Eleanor Roosevelt continued to serve as one of the nation's most influential first ladies, as a newspaper columnist and as one of her husband's most trusted advisers.

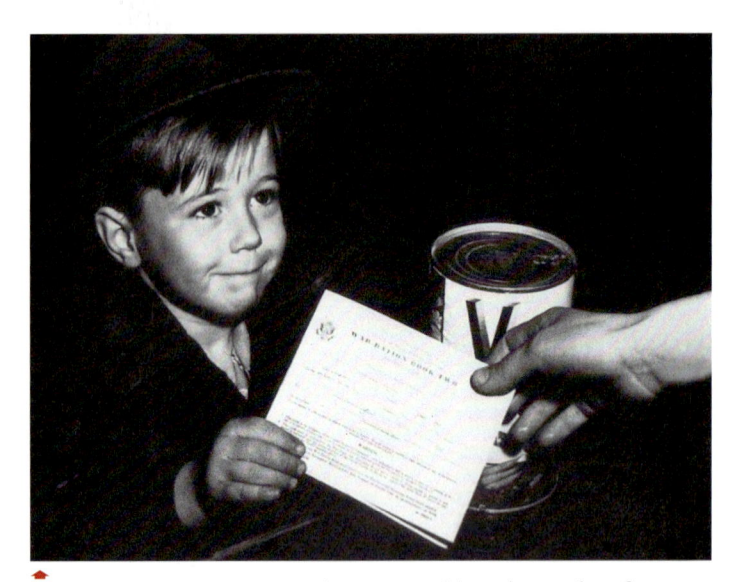

The Home Fronts: Allied and Axis Life During World War II

A young boy hands over his ration book to buy goods. Most foodstuffs and a wide range of other goods, such as clothes and shoes, were rationed.

Civilians were able to buy only a few gallons a week. New tires, spare parts, and new cars were largely unobtainable. All rubber and vehicle factories had switched to war production.

Raising war funds

Partly as a consequence of rationing and partly because of increased employment owing to the war effort, many people had surplus money they could not spend. The federal government targeted some of this money to pay for the war. Income taxes rose sharply, and the government borrowed tens of billions of dollars. Huge poster campaigns and rallies encouraged citizens to buy war bonds. These were savings certificates through which Americans loaned their savings to the government to raise money to fight the war in return for a set rate of interest.

The war economy

The demand for war equipment—tanks, planes, guns, ships, ammunition, uniforms, and other supplies—helped the U.S. economy overcome the effects of the Great Depression, which had lingered throughout the 1930s. The so-called New Deal of Franklin D. Roosevelt had aimed to provide employment and stimulate the economy. Nevertheless, at the start of the war in Europe in September 1939, U.S. unemployment was still above 15 percent. (Today an unemployment rate of 5 or 6 percent is considered normal.)

This image shows Flying Fortresses being built at a Boeing aircraft factory. During the war many companies switched their focus from consumer goods to military equipment.

The U.S. home front

CELEBRITIES IN THE WAR

Hollywood actors, musicians, and athletes were among the 14 million U.S. men who served during the war.

Famed band-leader Glenn Miller joined the U.S. Army Air Corps, where he conducted a band before dying in a plane crash late in the war. Movie star and future president Ronald Reagan became a captain in the Army Air Corps, though he did little more than appear in army training films during his service. Fellow movie star James Stewart was a bomber pilot and squadron commander on dangerous raids over Germany. Other movie stars to serve in the armed forces included Clark Gable, Henry Fonda, Gene Autry, and Douglas Fairbanks, Jr. Major-league baseball players made ideal celebrity soldiers, being young, in good shape, and accustomed to pressure. Ted Williams of the Red Sox, Joe DiMaggio of the Yankees, and Bob Feller of the Indians all served in the military during the war.

Even animated celebrities could serve the cause. Warner Brothers' Bugs Bunny and Daffy Duck squared off in cartoons against Hitler and the Japanese.

In 1942, Glenn Miller (left) became leader of the Glenn Miller Army Air Force Band.

As the United States prepared for possible war, millions of men left the workforce to join the military. Some volunteered, but others were drafted. At the same time, factories and farms needed more workers to increase productivity for the war effort. By 1943, unemployment had fallen to just over 1 percent, the lowest level ever measured in the United States.

As demand for armaments grew, U.S. companies switched from consumer production. Automotive giants General Motors (GM), Ford, and Chrysler began to produce military equipment: GM assembly lines turned out the M4 Sherman tank and the Avenger torpedo bomber in huge numbers. The new M3 submachine gun was made of simple stamped-metal parts. It was produced by companies that in peacetime made headlamps and jukeboxes.

The U.S. shipbuilding firm of Henry Kaiser could build a new cargo ship in 80 hours. Such ships were called Liberty ships, as they helped support the Allies' fight. They were built at a much faster rate than the German Navy could sink them. By the middle of the war, Allied armies and fleets went into battle knowing that they outnumbered the enemy in tanks, planes, and warships. The workers on the U.S. home front made a significant contribution to provide that decisive edge.

First steps in gender equality

In the 1940s, racial segregation and gender discrimination were still common. African Americans and other minorities

Boy Scouts deliver pots and other metal they have collected to a center in Brooklyn, NY. The metal was melted down to be used in weapons and ammunition.

were treated as second-class citizens. Women faced limited opportunities, especially in employment.

The situation was changed by the war. Almost all working-age white males were either in the military or already employed, so employers had to find other workers. Women had always played a huge role in running family farms, and jobs such as nursing and teaching were traditionally done by women. Prior to World War II, however, women had been largely excluded from working in factories and other jobs in the modern economy.

With a shortage of labor, however, women took on many traditionally male jobs. A famous poster campaign promoted a fictitious female worker named "Rosie the Riveter," who did an industrial job but did not become any less feminine. Some 30,000 women did high-paying but dangerous jobs in munitions factories. Women worked on assembly lines building ships and airplanes. The Kaiser firm employed so many women that it developed a comprehensive system of healthcare and childcare benefits.

Women also served as pilots, although not in combat. Pilots of the Women's Auxiliary Ferrying Squadron delivered aircraft from factories to air bases. Members of the Women's Army Auxiliary Corps (WAAC) and the Women Accepted for Volunteer Emergency Service (WAVES) traveled the globe to support U.S. bases overseas.

Racial emancipation

The war effort also helped open doors for ethnic minorities. African Americans were recruited into the military, but they were kept in segregated, all-black units. Most were forbidden from achieving full-combat status. Although they could become army officers, they were not put in positions where they could give orders to white troops. Hispanic Americans and Native Americans, on the other hand, were allowed to serve in integrated combat units.

At home, too, the war industry relied on racial minorities. But the closeness of white and nonwhite citizens caused great tension, as African Americans moved to cities to find work. Race riots broke out in Detroit during the war, and violence flared between whites and Hispanics in southern California.

No such luck

One group enjoyed no progress toward racial equality. At the start of the war, more than 100,000 Japanese Americans lived on the West Coast. After Pearl Harbor, many Americans saw them as a threat to national security.

In February 1942, Roosevelt issued Executive Order 9066. It ordered all

Japanese Americans to be removed from coastal areas, where they might be able to help a Japanese invasion. They were to be sent to camps. Some camps were in inland California and Arizona, but others were as far away as Arkansas.

The internment camps were isolated. They had few comforts, and the inmates were not free to leave. In some respects, the camps were run like small towns, with newspapers and a police force. Many camps began each day by singing the US national anthem.

The Japanese Americans felt that their internment was unnecessary and unjust. Most were American citizens, who had been born and raised in the United States. Many of the young Japanese American men sent to the camps later enlisted in the military. The all-Japanese American 442nd Regimental Combat Team fought in Italy. It became the U.S. Army's most decorated regiment.

Rosie the Riveter appeared in poster campaigns to encourage women to work in industry. She became an iconic image of female resolve.

Servicemen armed with clubs patrol the streets of Watts, Los Angeles, looking for Pachucos wearing zoot suits.

THE ZOOT SUIT RIOTS

The "zoot suit," a long and baggy jacket and pants, was an urban fad in the late 1930s and early 1940s. It caught on particularly among Mexican American teenagers in Los Angeles. These young "Pachucos" wore zoot suits and had long, slicked-back hair.

To servicemen in uniform, the zoot suits represented the civilian freedoms they were denied. Fights between servicemen and Pachucos often broke out in the streets of Los Angeles in 1942.

In June 1943, a rumor spread that a sailor had been beaten up by teens in zoot suits. More than 2,000 soldiers and sailors rampaged through Mexican neighborhoods of East Los Angeles. They roughed up hundreds of Pachucos and tore their zoot suits to shreds.

The military did little to punish the rioters. The Los Angeles City Council chose to blame the victims. It banned zoot suits in the city.

The Home Fronts: Allied and Axis Life During World War II

This female worker, employed at the 36th Street Airport in Miami, Florida, is welding a gasoline tank. During the war, many women took jobs that were traditionally the domain of men.

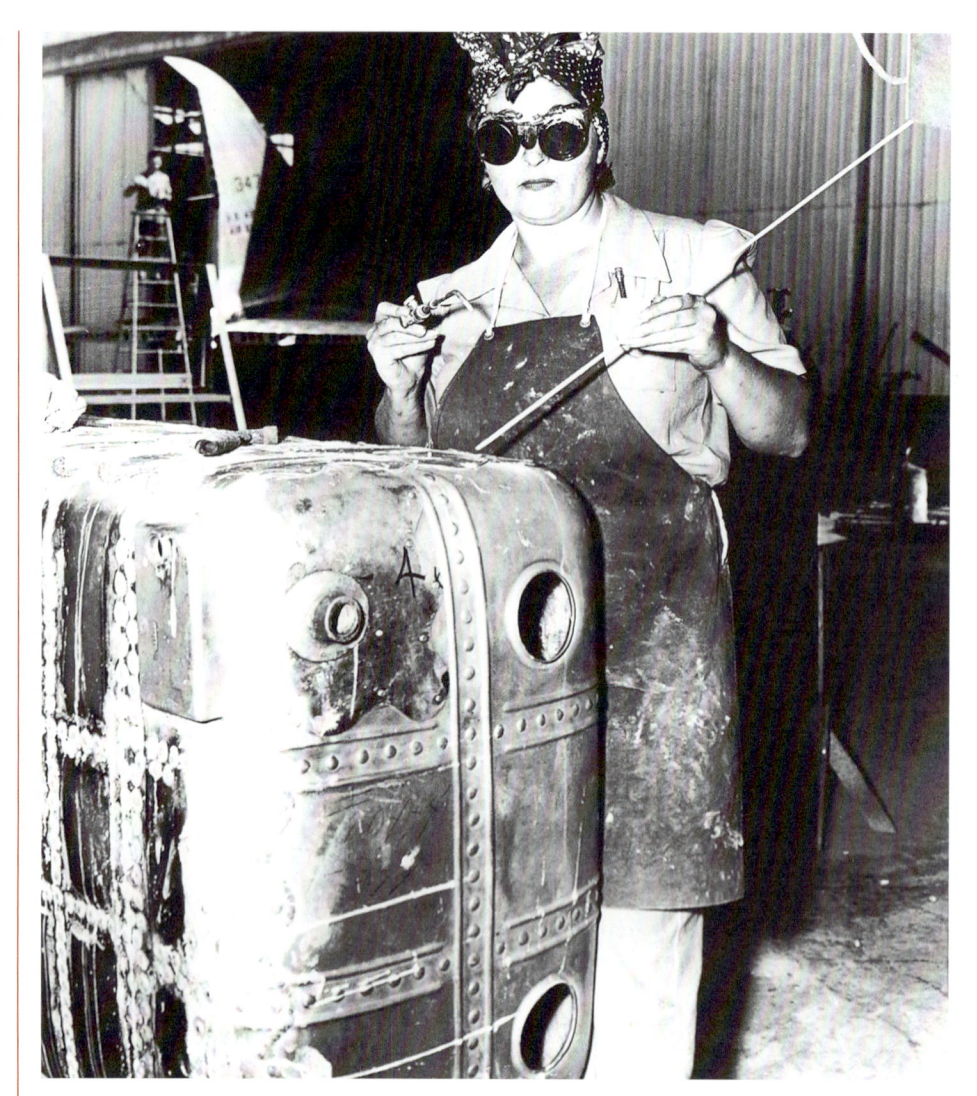

U.S. civilians escaped many of the hardships endured by the populations of other countries during the war, such as the Soviet Union, Poland, France, Germany, or Japan.

The war at home

The air raids feared at the start of the war never materialized. Rationing was inconvenient, but shortages did not reach the same levels as in other countries. Nevertheless, some traumas were as great for Americans as for any other combatants. Fourteen million men were in uniform, many of them serving overseas and in harm's way.

Their families lived with the fear that they would not return; around 300,000 servicemen never came back. Children grew up facing the absence of their fathers and sometimes their mothers.

Despite all the changes, some things carried on as usual. Major-league baseball stayed in business throughout the war. Hollywood produced movies emphasizing patriotic themes. Southern schools and businesses remained segregated, even for people in uniform.

Civilians were constantly reminded that the war was going on. Factories were plastered with posters warning workers that "Loose Lips Sink Ships!"

or encouraging them to produce more weapons and equipment for the front line. Letters to and from servicemen overseas were censored, removing any information that might be useful to the enemy.

Wartime propaganda

The accounts and images of the war that Americans received on the home front were carefully controlled by the government. The terror and horrific injuries that made up "real war" did not make it into Hollywood movies or newsreels. There were some exceptions. The public was horrified to see press images of dead Marines after the capture of Tarawa in the Pacific in November 1943. Correspondents like Ernie Pyle

Eyewitness Report:

"On March 23, 1943, while in class at Woodward High School, two FBI agents arrested me. I was interned when I was seventeen and released when I was twenty-two... Without experiencing internment, no one can appreciate the intense terror of government power and the despair of hopelessness and endless time one feels. In addition, an internee must suffer humiliation, stigmatization, and suspect 'friends' who may have given damning 'evidence' to the FBI, like whether one said something about Hitler when they were 12. Many bear the psychological scars throughout their lives. Many have gone to their graves never speaking of their internment to their families, my brother included. A large majority of internees still do not speak out."

From *My Internment by the US Government*, by German American Eberhard Fuhr

This image shows the branch office of the National Association for the Advancement of Colored People (NAACP) in Harlem, New York City. The war forced a change in attitudes toward ethnic minorities in the United States.

The Home Fronts: Allied and Axis Life During World War II

Americans of Japanese descent arrive at the Santa Anita Assembly Center in California on April 5, 1942. During World War II, thousands of Japanese Americans were forced from their homes into internment centers by Roosevelt's Executive Order 9066.

also tried to share with the U.S. public the realities of life for ordinary soldiers.

When the popular historian Studs Turkel published a book of interviews with hundreds of Americans who lived through World War II, he titled it *The Good War*. Several of the accounts were about the dark side of the wartime experience, including internment, censorship, segregation, and rationing. However, many of the interviews also touch on more positive elements of the wartime experience. They emphasized the progress made during the conflict. Turkel's interviewees believed that the country had benefited not only from defeating its powerful enemies, but also from social progress at home.

One element of that domestic progress was the movement toward racial and gender equality. Another was the development of an economy in which jobs were plentiful, well paid, and linked to other benefits. Other trends also emerged during the war that would shape later U.S. society.

Military bases and war production took place all over the United States, but the South and the west of the country received somewhat more than their share. In those areas, the war effort created new centers of growth and new expectations. The new social majority, the "middle class," expected to enjoy a good life, with benefits such as home ownership, a car,

POW CAMPS IN AMERICA: THE ENEMY AT HOME

Far from the fighting, the United States was a perfect site for prisoner-of-war (POW) camps. In 1943, Allied victories in North Africa and Sicily brought huge numbers of POWs from Europe. By December 1943, about 173,000 Axis prisoners were in U.S. camps. The number swelled to over 400,000 by the end of the war.

The prisoners were treated according to the rules laid down by international law. They were given food equal to that given to U.S. troops, and any labor they were forced to do was strictly limited. German prisoners were treated well in the hopes that the Nazis would treat their U.S. and British prisoners well in return.

Many Americans resented the captives. The Germans often had better food and lighter workloads than U.S. civilians themselves.

The situation changed at the end of the war. With no need to worry about Allied prisoners, and with full knowledge of the Holocaust, U.S. captors denied German prisoners their privileged status. Their conditions got much worse before they were returned to Germany.

The U.S. home front

THE GRUNTS' FRIEND

The most famous of U.S. war correspondents, Ernie Pyle traveled with U.S. troops in Europe and the Pacific. His reports from the frontlines were a welcome contrast to the version of the war seen in movie newsreels. The newsreels sanitized the war; they talked mainly about generals and commanders. Pyle wrote about the common soldiers, presenting them as they were: often bored, sometimes terrified, and almost always dirty and exhausted. Along with cartoonist Bill Mauldin, Pyle helped families back home understand what their young men in uniform were enduring. Americans saw the war as Pyle presented it, and shared his affection for the long-suffering "Grunts."

Pyle won the 1944 Pulitzer Prize for his wartime reporting. He also cooperated with the making of the 1945 propaganda movie, *The Story of GI Joe*, which was based on his accounts. Like so many of the GIs he wrote about, Pyle never made it home. He was killed by machine-gun fire during the invasion of the island of Ie Shima, off the coast of Okinawa, in April 1945.

Pyle offered the public a more truthful version of the war.

good schools, and the promise of an even better life for their children. The birth rate began to rise during the war; this was the start of the so-called baby boom of the 1950s and 1960s.

Before and after the war

It was not just the emerging communities of the "Sun Belt" that could look forward to a better future. The whole country had been changed by the war. In 1939, the United States was a nation still suffering from the effects of the Great Depression. During the 1930s, many Americans had wondered whether the best days of the nation had already gone. A few Americans even felt some admiration for the rapid economic growth of the dictatorships in Germany and Italy.

By 1945, in contrast, the United States was unquestionably the wealthiest and most powerful nation on the planet. While cities throughout Europe and Asia lay in ruins, urban centers in the United States were full of gleaming new buildings that showed off the nation's prosperity.

To many Americans, the United States was once more the land of good government and prosperity. Everyone had a job and enjoyed a comfortable lifestyle. To much of the rest of the world, World War II had brought devastation. To many Americans, however, it brought back the idea that the future belonged to the United States, and that it always would.

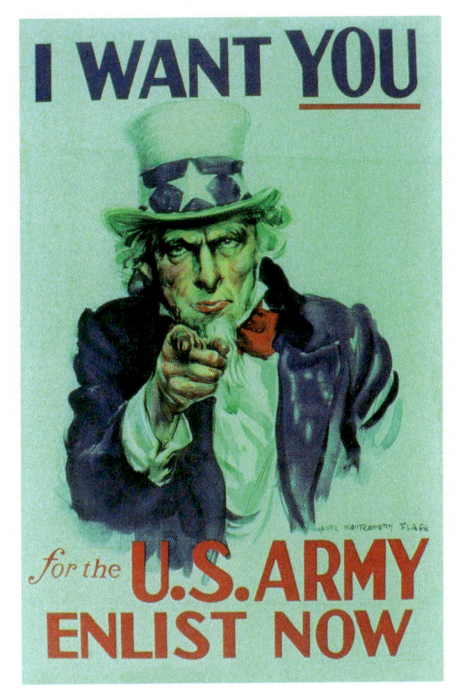

This famous image of Uncle Sam was painted by the artist James Montgomery Flagg.

15

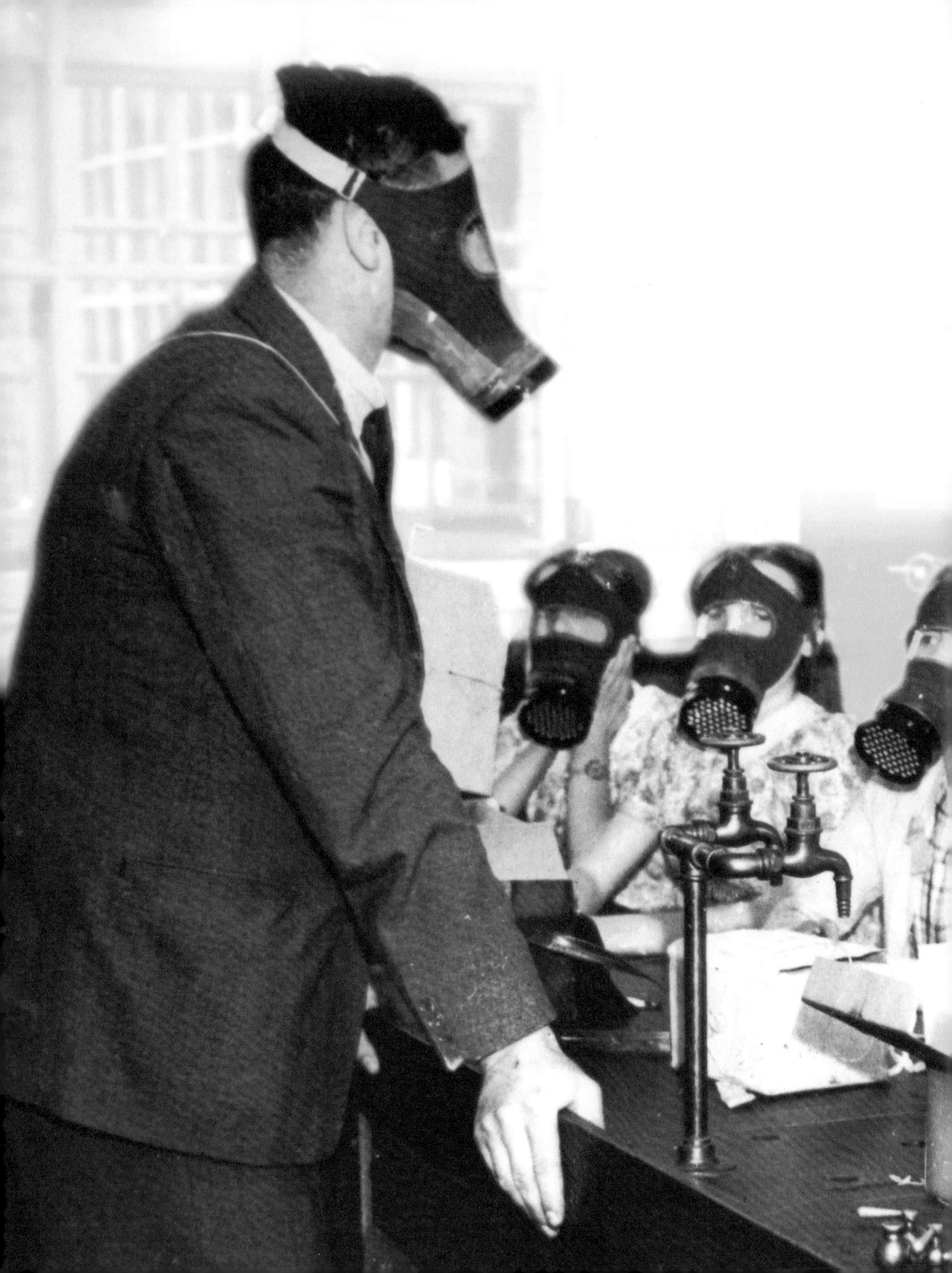

CHAPTER 2
ALLIED HOME FRONT: BRITAIN AND THE SOVIET UNION

The war transformed the social, economic, and cultural life of both Britain and the Soviet Union. The people of the Soviet Union, in particular, experienced great hardship during the war.

Previous pages: A British schoolteacher takes his pupils through a gas-mask drill in September 1939.

For Great Britain, the first few months of World War II were, in many ways, a huge anti-climax. On September 3, 1939, Prime Minister Neville Chamberlain went on the radio to tell the British that they were at war with Germany. The population prepared for the worst. They feared that there would be air raids, perhaps with bombs that released poisonous gas. For eight months, however, there were no air raids. Hitler's forces staged few major operations in western Europe. The conflict seemed so far away that the period became known as the "Phoney War."

The Phoney War

The British way of life changed, however. People prepared to be sheltered from bombs. In the cities, every family had to be able to get to an air-raid shelter. Local councils built thousands of concrete and brick shelters on streets or dug air-raid trenches in parks. In London, people could sleep on the platforms of the subway stations.

About a quarter of the population had back yards. They used outdoor shelters known as Anderson Shelters. These were named after the home secretary, John Anderson, who had them built. Anderson's engineers designed a simple shelter made from 14 sheets of corrugated iron. The sheets fit together to make a curved shell 6 feet (1.8m) high, 4.5 feet (1.4m) wide, and 6.5 feet (2m) long. The shelter was half-buried in the garden, and the roof was covered with a thick layer of earth. About 2.25 million Anderson Shelters were built during the war. They were issued free to poorer households.

Facing danger at home

When the bombing started, it turned out that the outdoor shelters sometimes caved in or collapsed under direct hits. As an alternative, from 1941 on an indoor shelter was introduced. It was named the Morrison Shelter after the new home secretary, Herbert Morrison. The new shelter looked like a huge,

This Anderson Shelter saved a family during a German air raid on the outskirts of London. A bomb made a crater right next to it.

very strong iron table. It had wire-mesh sides. The sides could be folded away, so that the shelter could be used as a table when there were no air raids. Morrison Shelters stood up even if heaps of rubble fell on top of them. They saved thousands of lives.

There were many other changes in British life. All citizens were given gas masks in case of a raid using poison gas. Even babies had special masks. A blackout was also brought in. It aimed to prevent German bombers from using streetlights or other lights to help them find their way to their targets. No light was allowed to show at night. People had to put up heavy shutters over every window and put out every light source when it got dark. Vehicles had to drive at night using only their sidelights. This resulted in such a dramatic rise in road accidents that blackout conditions were relaxed.

Living through the Blitz

By the middle of 1940, the Phoney War had become very real. U-boats in the Atlantic were sinking large numbers of merchant ships. That meant a huge shortage of food. The British had to cope with strict food rationing.

The dreaded air raids had also begun in 1940. The Luftwaffe, the German air force, first attacked the mainland with daylight raids against military targets. In September 1940, it began a series of night raids on key industrial cities, known as the Blitz. Citizens of cities such as London, Coventry, Plymouth, and Sheffield spent the night in air-raid shelters. The bombs thundered down around them. The tired inhabitants would emerge in the morning to see if their homes were still standing.

The Blitz had a great effect on British society. A total of 60,595 people were killed in air raids between 1939 and 1945. Another 86,182 people were injured. Hundreds of thousands of people were made homeless. More than one million city children were evacuated or sent to live with families in the countryside, where it was safer. They were separated from their own families and the people they knew. The experience was traumatic for both children and parents. But in some ways the policy was successful: two-thirds of evacuees eventually returned to their parents. Children made up only 7,736 of the civilian deaths in air raids.

This poster shows Adolf Hitler urging a mother to take her children back into the city. City children were sent to live in the country because it was safer. Both parents and children often found it difficult to be separated from their families.

Eyewitness Report:

> It was a night when London was ringed and stabbed with fire... Into the dark, shadowed spaces below us, while we watched, whole batches of incendiary bombs fell... They flashed terrifically, then quickly simmered down to pinpoints of dazzling white, burning ferociously. These white pinpoints would go out one by one, as the unseen heroes of the moment smothered them with sand. But also, while we watched, other pinpoints would burn on, and soon a yellow flame would leap up from the white center. They had done their work – another building was on fire. The greatest of all the fires was directly in front of us... Pinkish-white smoke ballooned upward in a great cloud, and out of this cloud there gradually took shape – so faintly at first that we weren't sure we saw correctly – the gigantic dome of St. Paul's Cathedral.

Ernie Pyle, U.S. war correspondent in London during the Blitz, 1940.

Changes in the workforce

In May 1940, the British government passed the Military Powers Act. The government took total control of employment. Since 22 percent of the workforce was in the armed forces, women were put to work on a bigger scale than ever before. A law of December 1941 made all women between the ages of 18 and 50 available for national service. They took on jobs in industry and agriculture. Women did many jobs that were usually done by men. They included welding, farming, working on the railroads, or driving buses, for example. The Women's Land Army was a labor organization formed in 1939 to work in agriculture. It had 80,000 members by 1944. More than 400,000 women also worked in

This picture from 1940 shows a man being extracted from the rubble of a bombed-out London building.

During the war years, production at the Spitfire factory in Castle Bromwich in central England increased by more than 700 percent.

RATIONING IN BRITAIN

A British poster urging people to recycle their kitchen waste to feed farmyard animals.

By 1941, almost every commodity was rationed in Britain. Most items had to be bought with ration coupons issued by the government. Soap, paper, new clothing, and gasoline were all restricted. The government encouraged people to cut down on all types of consumption. Posters intended to cut down on travel asked: "Is your journey really necessary?"

The slogan "Dig for Victory" encouraged people to grow fruit and vegetables. The campaign was highly successful. By 1943, there were 1.4 million vegetable gardens in Britain, up from 815,000 in 1939. Many families began keeping chickens and pigs for extra meat.

By mid-1942, regular weekly rations for an adult were about 1 pound (500 g) of meat, 8 ounces (250 g) of fats, 8 ounces (250 g) of cheese, some packets of dried eggs, and a small amount of jam. Bread, potatoes, vegetables, and fish were not rationed, but were not always available.

The ration system provided a balanced diet for everyone, something that the poor had not experienced before. However, the black market also thrived. Almost every family had a contact who could find them a few eggs, some extra meat, or a piece of cloth.

civil-defense roles. They were air-raid wardens or members of the Home Guard. Two million women worked in factories making weapons and ammunition. In all, about eight million British women were employed in the war effort.

Civilian men were also affected by the war. Many were called into service in vital war industries. Hundreds of thousands of coal miners were excused from military service. In December 1943, the British minister of labor, Ernest Bevin, drafted one in ten of all men aged between 18 and 25 for mine work. Conditions in the mines were dreadful: the wages were low, while fatalities from accidents were high. Miners went on

THE HOME GUARD

The Home Guard—known affectionately in Britain as "Dad's Army"—was originally named the Local Defense Volunteers (LDV). The LDV was created in May 1940. The new prime minister, Winston Churchill, felt there was a real threat of German invasion. He made a radio request for volunteers to form a national defense force. Within 24 hours, 250,000 men had signed up. By mid-June, LDV membership was more than one million. It stayed at that level for much of the war. In August 1940, Churchill renamed the LDV the Home Guard.

The Home Guard was intended to support regular army forces. It would man searchlights to search for aircraft at night. It would also perform guard duties, coastal patrols, and other tasks. If Britain was invaded, its members would become a guerrilla resistance force.

Manned mainly by older men and those exempt from military service, the Home Guard had only basic training and weapons such as shotguns or agricultural tools. Eventually they were issued rifles. Most were never called on to fight, although 140,000 served in anti-aircraft units. They did, however, perform a whole range of duties that took considerable pressure off regular fighting forces.

In the absence of army-issued rifles, a group of men enrolled in the Home Guard uses sticks during a drill in 1940.

Allied Home Front: Britain and the Soviet Union

THE AMERICAN "OCCUPATION"

In 1943, African American troops march through an English town singing a song and skipping in time.

Following the United States' entry into the war, about 1.5 million U.S. military personnel were stationed in the United Kingdom between 1942 and 1945. They were mainly U.S. Army and U.S. Army Air Force personnel. The Americans brought color to Britain's drab wartime existence, but also tension.

U.S. troops were well paid compared to British soldiers and had a seemingly limitless access to luxury goods. Such wealth, and the brash U.S. personality, made the GIs very attractive to young British women: some 60,000 would eventually marry Americans. British men felt they could not compete with the Americans' material advantages, and this led to animosity and occasional violence.

The British also saw unappealing sides of U.S. society. British civilians were shocked by the segregation of black and white troops in the U.S. Army. British pub landlords who served black soldiers would often see their bars wrecked by angry white GIs. However, the landlords almost always refused the white GIs' requests that they stop serving black men.

strike to protest against their conditions. Coal production actually fell by 25 million tons (25.4 million metric tonnes) between 1942 and 1945.

Most British people of working age found work during the war, except women with small children. The war brought long hours and many sacrifices. However, it also brought a standard of living that was in many ways an improvement on the Great Depression of the 1930s. Many people became enthusiastic volunteers in the war effort. Millions of citizens took on unpaid duties, ranging from air-raid warden to Home Guard soldier.

Britain's "finest hour"

Britain's efforts to keep its industry working led to an impressive increase in the output of factories. In 1939, for example, British factories produced 34,416 Lee-Enfield rifles; in 1943, that figure had risen to 909,785. In 1939, the

This window display in a Fifth Avenue store encouraged New Yorkers to support British industry by buying its goods.

23

The Home Fronts: Allied and Axis Life During World War II

THE GULAG

The gulag is the name given to a chain of prisons and labor camps set up in remote Siberia from about 1919. The name was an acronym of *Glavnoye Upravleniye Lagere*, or Administration of Corrective Labour Camps. Stalin sent anyone to the camps who remotely questioned or threatened his regime, or who fell foul of his paranoia. The victims ranged from peasant groups that Stalin said displayed "individualist tendencies" to intellectuals, writers, and artists.

The conditions in the gulag were harsh. In the Arctic Siberian winters, inmates were worked to death, or died from disease, starvation, or execution. By 1939, the camps held as many as 1.3 million people; another 800,000 were held in special penal colonies. During the war, thousands of inmates served in penal battalions. They were sent on operations that cost many lives, such as clearing minefields by walking through them. Between 1930 and 1950, at least a million people died in the gulag and the penal battalions. The camps officially closed in 1960, but some lasted into the 1980s.

Britain's industrial achievements were huge. British civilians all pulled together. They proved strong under attack from the Luftwaffe. Some historians call Britain's wartime period its "finest hour." However, not all sides of British life during the war were positive. Crime, for example, rose dramatically. There was much more theft and looting. The blackout made it easier for thieves. In 1939, there were around 300,000 crimes of all types committed in England and Wales, but in 1945 the figure had risen to 478,000.

The collectivization policy

For many Soviet citizens, the hardship of World War II was a continuation of pre-war conditions. The communist regime of Joseph Stalin had created many hardships for its citizens. In 1928, for example, it had introduced a policy of "collectivization." Soviet farmers were not producing enough grain to feed the population. Stalin forced small farmers to group together into large

British made 969 tanks; in 1942, as many as 8,611 tanks rolled off the assembly lines. In 1938, British factories produced 3,000 military aircraft. In 1944, the figure was 25,000. By that time, the aircraft industry employed 1.7 million people.

Women make munitions in a Moscow factory. With men engaged in the fight against the Germans, women were forced to take on roles usually reserved for men.

agricultural "collectives" in order to produce larger crop yields.

However, collectivization failed. Grain production remained low. Stalin sent five million small landlords to labor camps in Siberia and Central Asia as a punishment. Stalin's policy also created a famine that killed as many as 15 million Soviet peasants.

Facing massive losses

In spite of such hardships, the Soviet economy improved. When Germany invaded the Soviet Union in June 1941, it was one of the world's strongest military powers in terms of equipment. A total of 6,590 tanks and self-propelled guns had been produced in the first half of 1941 alone, along with 15,735 aircraft and nearly 68,000 artillery pieces.

Soviet industry had one major weakness. It was concentrated in

Soviet propaganda appealed to patriotism to defeat the Germans who had invaded the Russian homeland.

A Soviet female battalion marches through a village. Unlike in most other armies, many Soviet women fought on the frontline.

WOMEN IN THE SOVIET HOME FRONT

Soviet society changed greatly as a result of World War II. Following a government decree of February 1942, all women aged between 16 and 45 could be conscripted into war service. By 1945, 55 percent of the Soviet civilian workforce was female. That was an increase of more than 20 percent compared with 1941. Soviet women worked in all war industries, from armaments production to tank building. They were one of the highest-trained groups of the Soviet workforce.

Conditions for women in agriculture, however, were quite different. The Soviet government demanded higher grain quotas, but many men left agriculture to do military service. Millions of women struggled with land and livestock on their own.

Soviet women did not only fill the civilian roles of their male counterparts. They also served in the Soviet armed forces. About 800,000 females found themselves in frontline combat roles such as sniper, machine gunner, and fighter pilot.

The Home Fronts: Allied and Axis Life During World War II

Workers build tanks in a Soviet factory that has been moved to the Ural Mountains. Such factories operated around the clock.

the west of the country, which also contained most of the largest cities. Soviet factories were vulnerable to the German invasion from the west.

Fighting back

Stalin had not planned for the German invasion. When Germany invaded, however, the Soviets pulled off a remarkable achievement. As the Germans pushed into their country, Soviet workers dismantled 2,500 factories. They moved the equipment east by road and rail to the Ural Mountains, where they were out of harm's way. Then they rebuilt the plants and began production again. The move saved around 80 percent of Soviet war industry.

> "It was not uncommon to see people rather than horses pulling plows"

The human evacuation was equally enormous, since workers moved with the factories. As many as 25 million people may have headed east. They often traveled in poor conditions. Starvation cost thousands of lives.

Industrial achievements

The relocation of industry in 1941 helped save the Soviet Union from defeat in the months after the German invasion. Later, its industrial output increased until it exceeded that of Germany. In 1944, the peak year of Soviet war production, Soviet factories manufactured 40,200 aircraft, 29,000 tanks and self-propelled guns, 130,000 artillery pieces and mortars, and 2.5 million small arms. The Soviet Union also got large numbers of tanks, vehicles, and aircraft from its allies. The United States and the United Kingdom supplied equipment under a scheme known as Lend-Lease. By the end of the war, the Soviet Union had received nearly 22,000 aircraft and 12,500 tanks and self-propelled guns from its allies.

The hardships of civilian life

Life for Soviet civilians was hard. Supplies of clothing for civilians fell by around 80 percent between 1941 and 1945. Food production fell by between 30 and 40 percent across most food types. The average calorie intake fell to around 1,000 per day per person, less than half the usual amount. Workers toiled for up to 16 hours in factories, seven days a week. After their shifts, they often had to sleep in crowded and unsanitary housing units. Most heavy equipment and about half of all horses were diverted for military use, and millions of men were taken from the fields for army service. The farmers who remained had to work up to 20 hours a day. It was not uncommon to see people rather than horses pulling plows.

Stalin's rule

Soviet civilians also had to survive Stalin's continued persecution. Any dissent or opposition to the government resulted in arrest by the NKVD, Stalin's internal security organization. Dissenters were usually imprisoned in the gulag camps or executed. On occasion, Stalin ordered the forced deportation of entire peoples whom he felt were politically unreliable. More than 520,000 Chechens and Ingushetians from the Caucasus region were sent east in February 1944. In the same year, 180,000 Crimean Tartars were deported. The deportations were conducted with great brutality. They still cause tensions in the region today.

Life under occupation

Conditions were even worse for Soviet civilians under German occupation. There were also millions of civilians caught up in besieged cities. They were killed by bombing raids or by artillery attacks, or they died from disease. Communist Party officials, Jews, and suspected partisans, or resistance fighters, were murdered by Nazi execution squads. A total of 1,700 cities and towns were damaged or destroyed by the war, leaving millions homeless.

During the German blockade of Leningrad, which began in September 1941, workers were rationed to 9 ounces (225g) of bread a day. They ate dogs and cats, as well as horse meat. For months, the city had no electricity or fuel for heating or transportation. Weak or sick people fell dead in the streets. Unburied bodies spread diseases. The siege lasted for 900 days. About 630,000 civilians died from cold and starvation. Another 200,000 died in German air raids.

Conclusion

Up to 25 million Soviet citizens died between 1939 and 1945. More than half the dead were civilians. (In contrast, the United States and Britain lost around 300,000 people each.) Caught between the German invaders and the actions of their own leader, the Soviet people suffered an almost unparalleled degree of horror during World War II.

This 1941 photograph shows a hungry Soviet couple hunting for possible food among discarded potato skins near a factory destroyed by the retreating Red Army.

CHAPTER 3
AXIS HOME FRONTS

Prior to the twentieth century, wars were principally a matter of defeating the enemy's armies on the battlefield. World War II, however, fully involved the world's civilian populations.

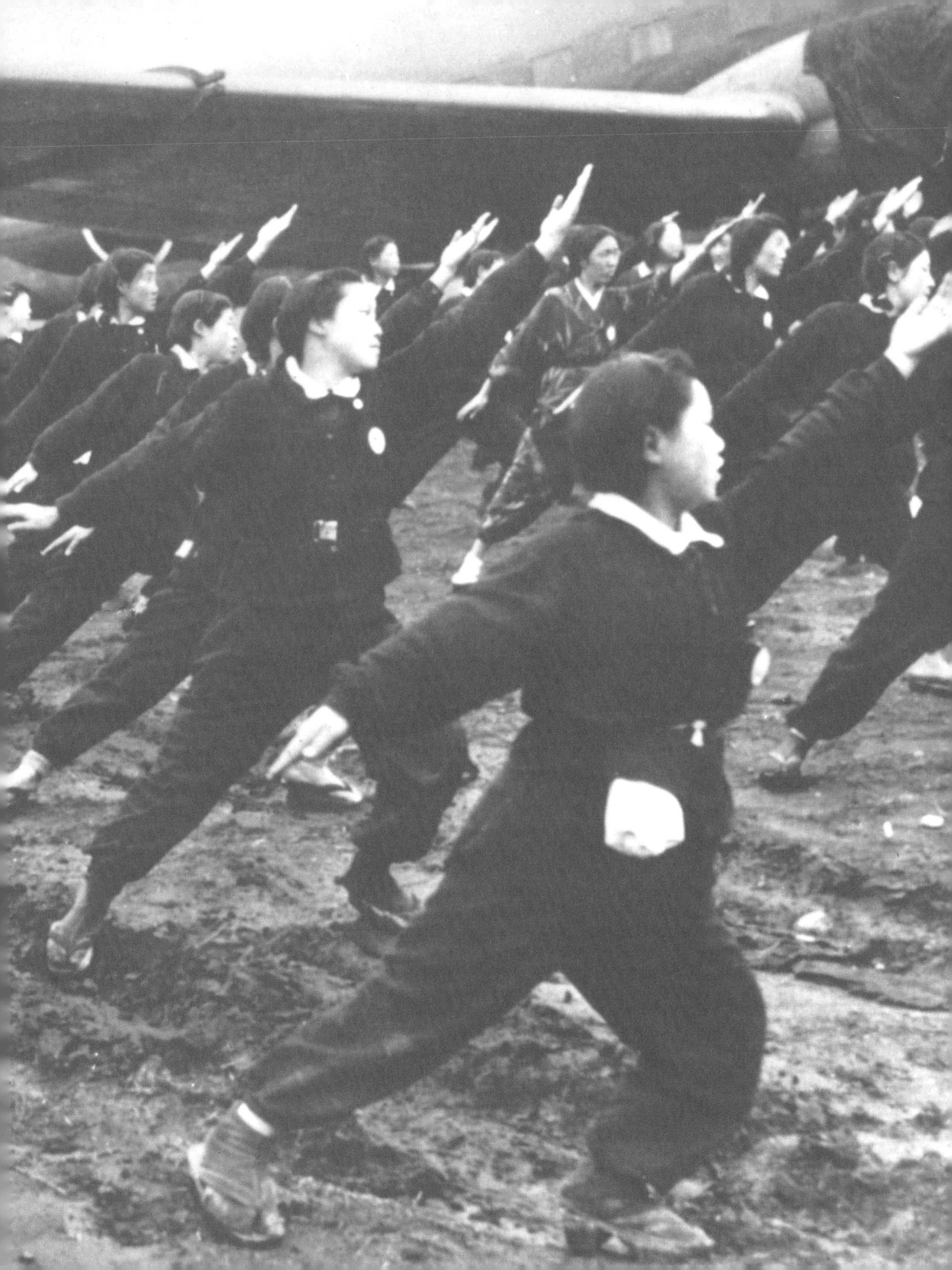

Previous pages: This 1942 photograph shows Japanese women exercising before going to work.

Between 1939 and 1941, the German people noticed little change in their standard of living, despite the war. Nearly everyone had jobs. The Nazi government had greatly increased the number of posts for civil servants. Such jobs were relatively well paid. Factories kept making luxury and consumer goods. Germans spent only 20 percent less on leisure and entertainment in 1941 than in 1938. This was all to change in 1942.

Deepening crisis

The rapid German victories of 1939 and 1940 masked a weak Nazi war economy. During the 1930s, Hitler had prepared the state and military for *blitzkrieg* ("lightning war"). He had not prepared for a war drawn out over several years. By late 1941, Germany's offensive into Russia had ground to a halt near Moscow, and the war in North Africa was turning against the Axis. The German Army was stretched from Scandinavia to Libya and from the English Channel to Moscow. The scale of the war used huge reserves of manpower, raw materials, and money. Rationing had been introduced in 1939. Now it really started to bite. Coal, soap, and gasoline were restricted. Most clothing production was diverted to make military uniforms. Food was also rationed. The situation got worse later in the war. The Allies began bombing German factories, and the territory occupied by Germany began to get smaller.

Women join the war effort

German society changed as dramatically as the standard of living. In 1939, the German workforce of 39 million included 37 percent female workers and 4.5 million men in military uniform. The Nazi Party had a traditional view of women. It encouraged them to be homemakers. Despite protests from the military high command, the Nazis initially resisted bringing women into the workforce. The number of female workers actually declined from September 1939 to May 1941.

That changed from February 1942, when Albert Speer became minister for armaments and war production. Supported by Fritz Sauckel, who was put in charge of the mobilization of labor, Speer began gearing the economy for total war. Between 1942 and 1945, he and Sauckel reshaped society. They had to cope with a severe shortage of workers caused by the Eastern Front's enormous drain on manpower at home.

By 1944, the German armed forces had swelled to 10.5 million

Eyewitness Report:

" Having to go to work over piles of rubble and through clouds of dust; the impossibility of washing oneself properly or of cooking at home because there was no water, gas, or electricity;... the difficulty of shopping for food because most of the shops had been destroyed or had closed of their own accord; the continual explosions of delayed-action bombs or duds;... the delay in postal deliveries, the stopping of newspapers;... the disappearance of every means of relaxation such as the cinema, theater, concerts, etc. "

Official report from the city of Aachen, describing the experiences of residents during bombing campaigns

This photograph shows a horse-drawn cart transporting vital provisions of grain from Ukraine to Germany. Following the Nazi–Soviet agreement, Ukraine provided the Third Reich with food supplies from 1940 until June 1941.

FOOD RATIONING IN GERMANY

During the course of the war, German civilians experienced a dramatic tightening of food rationing. In 1939, an adult received an unlimited ration of bread, 19 ounces (550 g) of meat, and 11 ounces (300 g) of fats (butter and lard) each week. By October 1942, the allowances had been reduced to 74 ounces (2,125 g) of bread, 12 ounces (350 g) of meat, and roughly 7 ounces (200 g) of fat.

Rationing got even worse. The lowest point came in April 1945, the penultimate month of the war, when the ration consisted of just 32 ounces (900 g) of bread, 5 ounces (137 g) of meat, and 3 ounces (75 g) of fats.

The tight rationing meant that the black market (the illegal sale of goods) flourished even more. This further undermined the German economy.

This German ration card shows what the citizens of the Reich were entitled to: bread, meat, butter, and grains.

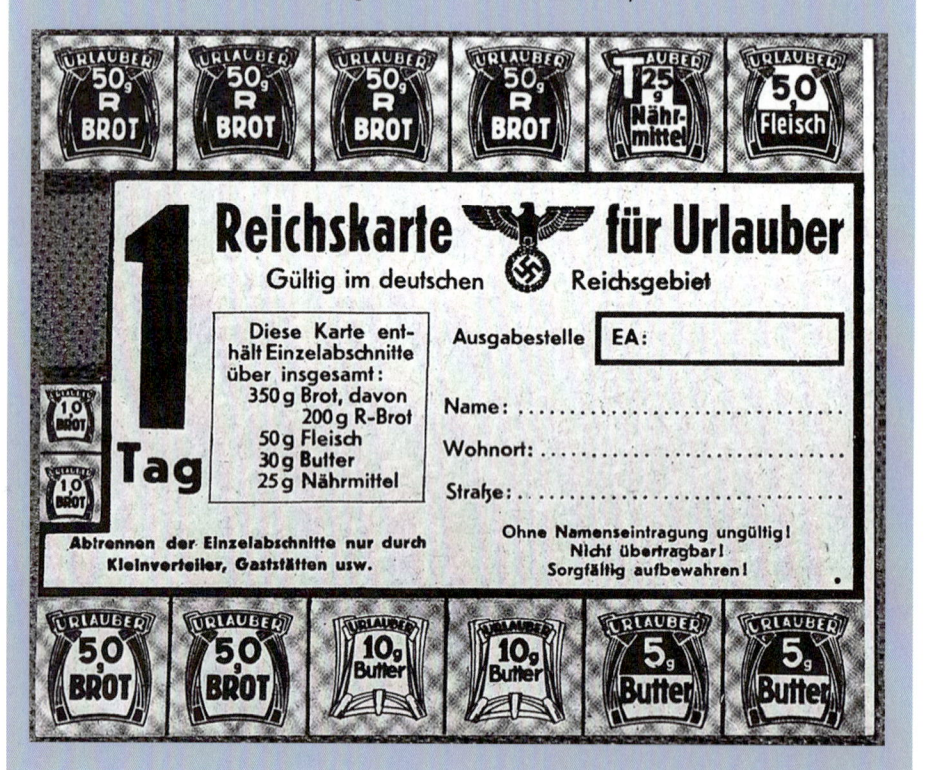

men. On February 18, 1943, the Nazi propaganda minister Joseph Goebbels announced that, following the crushing German defeat at Stalingrad, Germany would now fight a total war. All able-bodied Germans would contribute to the defeat of the Allies. By 1944, women made up more than 50 percent of the civilian workforce. However, they still did not play as important a role as women did in the industries of other nations, such as Great Britain.

Every male civilian between 16 and 65 years old was signed up to compulsory labor schemes. Members of the Hitler Youth were also employed in a wide range of civil and military positions. Boys as young as 15 years were manning anti-aircraft guns around German cities from 1943. The number of foreign workers also rose tremendously. They included slave laborers, prisoners of war, and regular workers from the countries occupied by Germany. By August 1944,

In Germany, the entire population contributed in their own way to the war effort. Women were typically put to work making uniforms, as shown here.

7.8 million foreign workers were toiling for the Third Reich. Hundreds of thousands were worked to death.

Steady industrial output

Nazi Germany achieved some remarkable increases in production. In 1940, German factories made 2,200 new tanks; in 1944 that figure had risen to 27,300. Some 787,000 artillery pieces were produced in 1944, compared with 171,000 in 1939. Most impressively, whereas the German Air Force (the *Luftwaffe*) received 3,865 new aircraft in 1939, in 1944 it received some 39,800. People worked 12-hour days, seven days a week. Such industrial achievements continued, despite a string of defeats, massive Allied bombing, and restricted manpower. It was not until the very last months of the war, when the Allies invaded Germany itself, that industrial output fell.

German propaganda

The Nazis used propaganda to help preserve national unity, until Germany's final defeat became undeniable.

Goebbels tightly controlled the press. He staged great rallies to convince people of Germany's continuing strength. Nazi publications such as *Der Angriff* ("The Attack"), *Signal*, and *Die Wehrmacht* (named after the German armed forces) promoted the idea of German military supremacy. Goebbels continued his propaganda even in the face of huge defeats, such as Stalingrad in the winter of 1942–43.

Propaganda could not lessen the impact of the Allied bombing campaign, which grew more intense after 1942. By the war's end, Germany's city dwellers were living under air raids that came night and day. In total, around 305,000 German civilians died in the attacks, and a further 800,000 were injured.

More than five million people were left homeless when they

Goebbels was famous for his impassioned speeches, which he used to rally the people of Germany to support the war effort.

German civilians and Hitler Youth members wait to perform compulsory labor, such as digging defenses.

ALBERT SPEER (1905–1996)

Albert Speer was born on March 15, 1905, and went on to study architecture. He joined the Nazi Party in 1931, becoming a member of the SS the following year. He rose to fame as a designer of huge Nazi rallies in 1933 and 1934. On these occasions, Speer used vast arrangements of people, flags, Nazi symbols, and searchlights to create images of overwhelming power. In 1937, Speer became Adolf Hitler's personal architect and city planner as the Reich's general architectural inspector.

When war began, Speer's appointments became more political. In 1942, he was appointed minister of armaments and war production, and set about energizing Germany's military industries. He later held a series of other important offices. In the last days of the war, Speer tried to prevent Hitler's order that all German infrastructure be destroyed.

During the Nuremberg Trials in 1946, where he was charged with war crimes, Speer admitted his guilt. He served 20 years' imprisonment, and he later published the book *Inside the Third Reich*. Speer died in 1996.

Speer's reputation was made by his architectural visions for the Reich.

fled some two million bombed houses. Entire cities, such as Dresden and Hamburg, were almost completely destroyed. Life during the air raids was traumatic.

By the end of the war, when defeat was already inevitable, Germans also faced increasing brutality from their own government. The Nazi police and SS organizations locked up or executed anyone critical of Hitler's regime.

Life in Italy

Like Germany, Italy experienced the grim realities of rationing: poor wages, long working hours, and Allied bombing. However, Italians were in many ways less committed to the war than the Germans. The Nazi Party imposed unity on the German people. Mussolini's fascist regime, however, had attracted opposition movements from when it first took power. The war served to sharpen the country's social divisions.

Italy was broadly split in two. The north was wealthier, with industrial cities such as Turin and Milan. The agricultural south was far worse off.

War made life difficult for both groups. Around two million

Young musicians celebrate Hitler's birthday in 1944. Such displays were intended to boost German morale.

The Home Fronts: Allied and Axis Life During World War II

OPPOSITION IN GERMANY

Opposition to Hitler within German society was limited, but there were exceptions. Communists and socialists, traditional enemies of the Nazis, formed several resistance groups. The Uhrig-Römer Group, for example, produced resistance literature. The Red Orchestra network of communist spies provided intelligence for the Soviets. Some 30,000 left-wing activists were executed between 1933 and 1945.

Resistance was also found elsewhere. The White Rose group was formed by students at Munich University. They protested against the treatment of the Jews, which had been witnessed at first hand by some of its members. The Kreisau Circle, a group of military officers and business leaders, formed an underground intellectual resistance movement. Christian resisters included Dietrich Bonhöffer, a leading member of the Protestant Confessional Church. After speaking out against Nazi policies, he was arrested in April 1943 and executed on April 9, 1945.

In July 1944, Hitler survived an assassination attempt by high-ranking German Army officers; this was the closest any resistance came to threatening the Nazi regime.

Three of the five members of the White Rose group: (left to right) Hans Scholl, Sophie Scholl, and Christoph Probst.

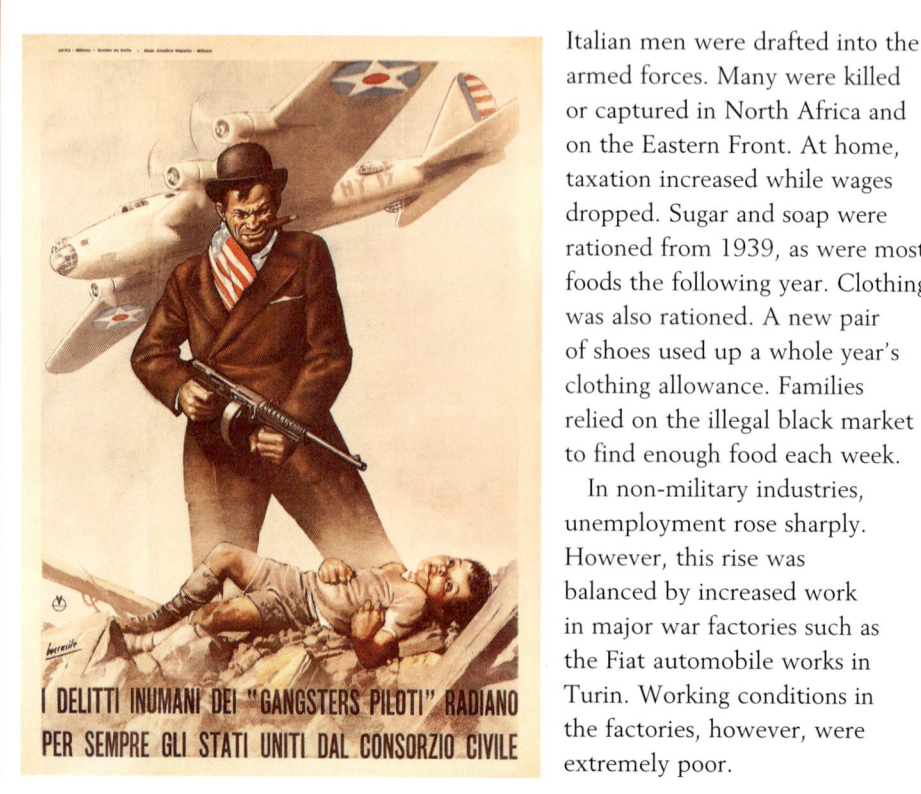

This Italian poster shows an American "bandit" leering over the body of a child killed in an Allied bombing raid.

Italian men were drafted into the armed forces. Many were killed or captured in North Africa and on the Eastern Front. At home, taxation increased while wages dropped. Sugar and soap were rationed from 1939, as were most foods the following year. Clothing was also rationed. A new pair of shoes used up a whole year's clothing allowance. Families relied on the illegal black market to find enough food each week.

In non-military industries, unemployment rose sharply. However, this rise was balanced by increased work in major war factories such as the Fiat automobile works in Turin. Working conditions in the factories, however, were extremely poor.

In March 1943, the country was gripped by a series of major strikes.

The loss of male workers

Matters were even worse in the countryside. During the war, many people moved from the country to the towns for work. Many men had already been drafted into the military. Rural communities lost many of their male workers. Peasant families were already poor. Many had only just enough to eat. Now they faced disaster. They had fewer workers, but the government demanded that they produce more grain. In 1943, the government targeted sharecroppers, who farmed land for a landowner. They had to give the landowner a share of the harvest in place of rent. Now the government also made them contribute grain to state granaries. This was a terrible burden on the rural population.

By 1943, Italy was heading for social collapse. Economically, the country had limited natural resources. Its output of aircraft and tanks was small compared with that of most of the other combatants. The national budget could barely pay the huge military expenditure. The cost of supporting the armed services between 1936 and 1940 alone was $72.3 million.

Italy changes sides

Change came in a dramatic form after the Allies invaded the Italian island of Sicily on July 10, 1943. The government rebelled against Mussolini. On July 25, King Victor Emmanuel III fired the dictator. Marshal Pietro Badoglio took over the government.

Several months of political turmoil followed as Badoglio's government held secret peace talks with the Allies. Hitler was furious at the prospect of losing his ally. On September 3, however, Badoglio signed an armistice with the Allies. Under the agreement, Italy became a "co-belligerent" of the British and U.S. forces, meaning that it had effectively changed sides. The Germans moved fast to occupy as much

Italian women help finish off new cars at the Fiat works in Turin in 1940. Such factories were later switched to war production.

The Home Fronts: Allied and Axis Life During World War II

POPE PIUS XII AND THE NAZIS

Pope Pius XII was in the Vatican for the duration of the conflict.

The relationship between Pope Pius XII and the Nazis still generates intense controversy. Cardinal Eugenio Pacelli was elected pope in March 1939. As a cardinal, in July 1933, he had signed an agreement with Germany. It included a commitment to "consolidate and develop the amicable relations existing between the Holy See (the church) and the German Reich."

Critics have argued that Pius XII did not condemn the Nazi regime enough. In particular, they say, he was guilty of cowardice because he remained virtually silent on the subject of the Holocaust.

However, Pius XII did push for a negotiated end to the war. In June 1943, he criticized the murder of the Jews, albeit in general terms. His aid organizations also rescued thousands of Jews. Although the pope's statements against the war and genocide enraged the Nazis, the Allied governments believed they did not go far enough.

---

of Italy as they could. By the end of September, Italy was split between the German-controlled north (from Naples northward, including Rome) and the Allied-occupied south. Life was hard on both sides of the line.

These Italian women are knitting clothing for their country's soldiers. Such efforts were typical throughout the war.

North and south

The Italians living under German control, for example, suffered repression and cruelty. The Germans began sending Jews from northern Italy to death camps, where they were killed. Other Italians were recruited as forced labor. There was much public resistance to the Germans. When they tried to conscript most of Naples' young males in September 1943, street fighting broke out. It left 162 Neapolitans dead. The death toll would have been worse if the Allies had not liberated the city by the end of the month. The Germans also had to face strikes. In March 1944, for example, 300,000 workers in Milan struck against occupation policies.

Italians living under Allied control also faced hardship. The Allies' steady

After bombing a store, this group of Italian partisans point their guns at a suspected pro-fascist who has been pulled from inside. This photograph was taken in 1944.

advance through Italy cost many Italian lives and destroyed roads, homes, and whole towns. Allied financial policies pushed up prices and reduced the value of the local currency. The Allies seized food supplies, causing hunger and even starvation among Italian civilians. Naples was particularly badly hit. By the time the Allies liberated the city, Allied bombing had left 200,000 citizens homeless. In July 1944, only 3.4 percent of the goods stored in Naples was available to ordinary Italians in the form of rations.

In the north, meanwhile, unofficial Italian forces began to attack the Nazis. These guerrilla forces, called partisans, were often former soldiers. Some 40,000 partisans died in attacks on German positions, but they made a great contribution to the war effort.

Japanese life

In many ways, Japan had been on a war footing since the early 1930s, when it began an ongoing conflict with China. Military expenditure grew steadily from 1931. In 1940, the year before its attack on Pearl Harbor, Japan spent 66 percent of its total national budget on the armed services.

When the war began, Japan's economy struggled because of the country's lack of natural resources. Japan relied heavily on imports of everything from metals and petroleum to rice. Between 1941 and 1944, however, Japanese industry managed to increase its production of military equipment. The greatest achievements were in aircraft production. In 1941, 5,088 aircraft of all types were built; in 1944, that figure had risen to 28,180. The increase in production partly reflected the fact that, as Japan suffered more defeats on land, air defense became of greater importance. The production of tanks fell by more than 90 percent during the same period.

> "In 1940, Japan spent 66 percent of its total national budget on the armed services"

Economic and social collapse

As the war went on, U.S. naval and air power slowly strangled the Japanese war economy by cutting off its imports. In 1945, the economy collapsed. Aircraft output fell to just over 6,000 airplanes. The production of aircraft carriers,

This Japanese propaganda poster was aimed at U.S. troops, or "Doughboys." It was intended to scare them by threatening that they would be killed in action.

battleships, and cruisers stopped altogether. Economic disintegration went hand in hand with social chaos. U.S. air raids inflicted great damage on Japanese towns and cities, where only starvation rations were available. Thousands of workers moved into the countryside to seek food and safety. Industry lost many of its key workers, so war production fell even quicker.

The economic collapse of 1945 was the final straw, but Japanese society had been living with shortages since the late 1930s. Various national bodies had been created to keep the Japanese people committed to the war, despite the hardships it brought. Japanese civilians of all ages were overseen by organizations such as the Industrial Patriotic League, the Imperial Rule Assistance Association, the Greater Japan Youth Corps, and the Greater Japan Women's Association.

Such organizations had officials at every level of Japanese society. Japanese life was increasingly stripped of all luxuries. The government attempted to harden society for total war. Young boys were sent to classes that taught them about Japan's military ideology. Social venues such as bars had their opening hours cut to prevent frivolous enjoyment. Consumer goods with Western names were relabeled with Japanese names. Even the sending of telegrams was forbidden by the communications ministry. From September 1939, the first day of every month was a "Public Service for Asia Day." Citizens had to work for free on government projects.

The militarization of Japan

Japanese society became more militarized as the war went on. The conflict began well for Japan, but after the defeat in the Battle of Midway in 1942, Japan was on the defensive. The government widened conscription to include groups of men who had previously been exempt from military service. On October 21, 1943, at the Meiji Shrine Stadium, 25,000 university students were given a public send-off to military service. They were armed only with wooden rifles, however, because there were production shortages of guns.

From September 1943, single women aged between 18 and 25 were conscripted into the Japanese labor corps. They worked in agriculture and industry. In 1945, civilians were formed into People's Volunteer Units. They were trained to support the regular military if the United States eventually invaded mainland Japan.

Food shortages

One of the worst problems for Japanese civilians was hunger. They suffered under some of the strictest rationing of the war. Even at maximum production, Japan still needed to import 22 percent of its rice, which was the staple food in the Japanese diet. It also had to import 82 percent of its sugar.

The government controlled rice distribution from 1939. By 1944, most other foods were also tightly rationed. By the end of 1944, many adults had to survive on only a handful of vegetables

In 1941, a Tokyo businessman is driven around by a bicycle taxi. These vehicles were introduced because of the gasoline shortage resulting from Japan's war with China.

and 8 ounces (225 g) of rice each day. Most people got no meat, although some occasionally ate fish; some even ate cats and dogs. In the last months of the war in 1945, when the Allied blockade of Japan was total, many people no longer had rice rations. Starvation and disease were rampant in the cities.

Japanese civilians also suffered from the effects of the Allied bombing campaign from late 1944. In just one raid on Tokyo, on March 9, 1945, U.S. B-29 bombers killed more than 100,000 people. They dropped incendiary bombs intended to start fires. The bombs began a firestorm that raged through the wooden houses. The atomic bombs of August 1945 were the culmination of a highly destructive campaign using conventional bombs.

Deadly ambitions

At the start of the war, none of the Axis powers were prepared for a long, drawn-out conflict, particularly not one against the industrial might of the United States. In Germany, Italy, and Japan, civilians paid dearly for their leaders' ambitions and their own complicity in those ambitions.

JAPAN'S MOBILIZATION OF YOUTH

As in Nazi Germany, Japan's war effort involved preparing children for military service. In 1941 the government established the Greater Japan Youth Corps (GJYC) to oversee Japanese schools. The GJYC changed the school curriculum. Book learning became less important than military-style training.

Training could be brutal. Boys as young as eight played "national defense sports." Teams competed against one another in physically strenuous games in which any signs of weakness were punished. Children were often dressed in military uniforms and taught military drill. In the classroom, they were instructed in military theory and anti-Western history.

The training paid off. In 1945, with the war closing in on the Japanese home islands, significant numbers of children in their mid-teens fought on the island of Okinawa. They suffered overwhelming losses.

CHAPTER 4
LIFE IN OCCUPIED EUROPE

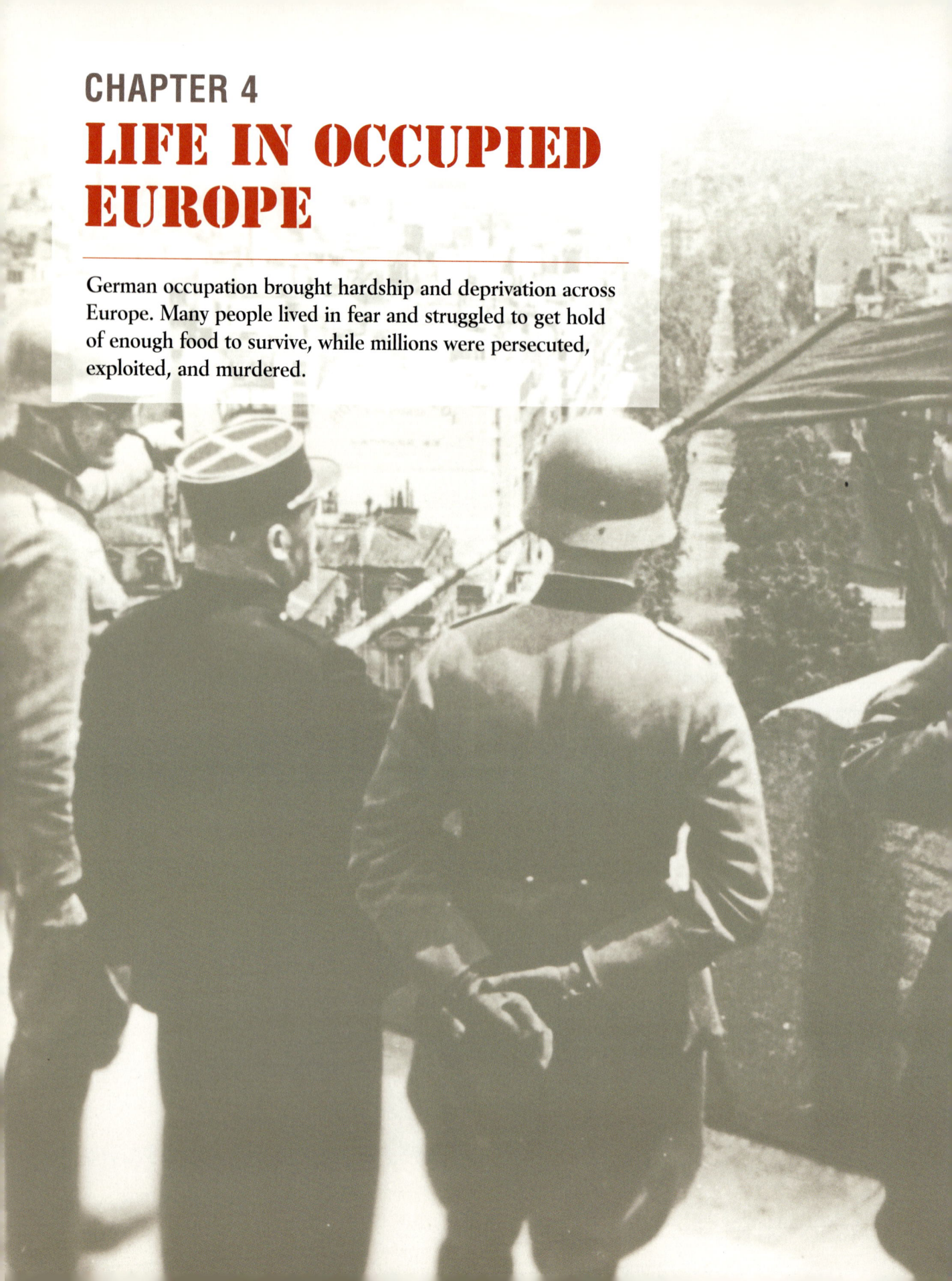

German occupation brought hardship and deprivation across Europe. Many people lived in fear and struggled to get hold of enough food to survive, while millions were persecuted, exploited, and murdered.

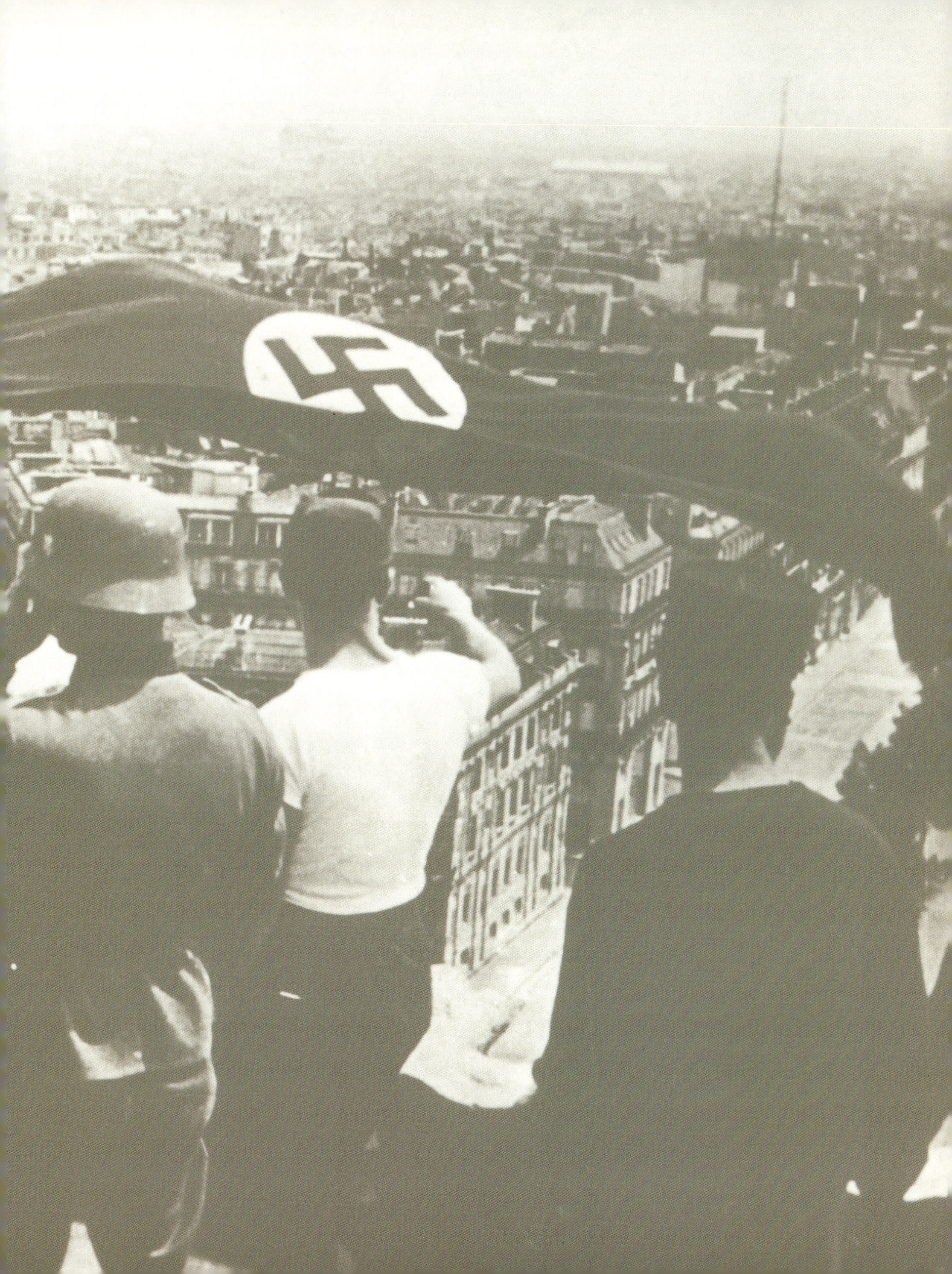

Young men in the Czech capital, Prague, look at a German poster advising them to join the SS. Thousands of men in occupied countries joined the German forces.

Previous pages: German soldiers and French officials look on from the roof of the Arc de Triomphe as the Nazi swastika flies over Paris on June 17, 1940. German troops entered the French capital on June 14; they occupied the city until August 1944.

By the end of 1942, the Germans had defeated and occupied Belgium, Holland, France, Denmark, Luxembourg, Norway, Greece, Poland, Yugoslavia, Latvia, Lithuania, and Estonia. Hitler's forces also occupied a huge part of the western Soviet Union. Hundreds of millions of people were under Nazi rule.

Hitler's conquests presented many problems. The occupied territories and all their diverse peoples had to contribute to the good of Germany. In July 1941, Hitler told his High Command: "We now have to face the task of cutting the giant cake according to our needs, in order to be able, first, to dominate it, second, to administer it, and third, to exploit it." Hitler was referring to recent German advances in the Soviet Union. His objectives, however, applied to all conquered regions. His main aim was to strip each occupied country of its economic and natural resources for the benefit of Germany.

Under German rule

The political arrangements in the occupied countries varied widely. Denmark, for example, was allowed to keep its existing political framework, albeit under heavy supervision from Germany. Christian X remained king, and the major political parties formed a coalition government on July 8, 1940. The arrangement ceased in August 1943. Faced with increasing Danish opposition, Hitler replaced the government with a German Reich commissioner.

In Norway, the Germans installed a series of governments, culminating in one headed by Vidkun Quisling. Quisling was a Norwegian politician who had long collaborated with the Germans. His surname later became a term of abuse for any kind of traitor.

France, Hitler's most prestigious conquest, was split in two after the French surrender on June 21, 1940. Northern and western France was put under direct German military occupation. Southern France was not occupied, but was governed from the town of Vichy. The Vichy government collaborated with the Nazis. It was led by the French officer and World War I hero Marshal Philippe Pétain. The arrangement lasted until November 11, 1942. After the Allied victories in Africa just across the Mediterranean sea from Vichy, the Germans feared that Vichy France would become a strategic risk. Hitler ordered his troops to occupy it.

The Germans kept many of the existing systems of government in the occupied countries of northern and western Europe.

German tactics

Although the national governments seemed to have some degree of power, in reality authority lay with Nazi officials. In Norway, for example, although Vidkun Quisling was minister president, the country was really governed by Reich Commissioner Josef Terboven. Terboven was much hated by Norwegians, particularly for his persecution and extermination of many of the country's Jews.

The conquered territories in southern and eastern Europe had no illusions about who was in charge. In Greece, the

A German officer watches enslaved Jewish workers in Poland in July 1941. Three million Polish Jews were killed during the German occupation. Most of them were worked to death or gassed in extermination camps.

The Home Fronts: Allied and Axis Life During World War II

PHILIPPE PÉTAIN (1856–1951)

Philippe Pétain was chief of state of the French Vichy government. He was born in 1856 and joined the French Army in 1876. By the outbreak of World War I in 1914, he had risen to the rank of colonel. In 1916, he was made commander-in-chief of French forces on the Western front. Popular with soldiers and civilians alike, Pétain became the French war minister in 1934. In May 1940, the French premier, Paul Reynaud, appointed Pétain minister of state as the country collapsed under the German invasion. Pétain argued against resistance, and when he replaced Reynaud on June 16, he arranged an armistice with Germany. Pétain set up a collaborationist government at Vichy in central France. After the defeat of Germany in May 1945, Pétain was tried as a war criminal. Found guilty, he was sentenced to death. He was reprieved and spent the rest of his life as a prisoner until he died at the age of 95.

Pétain was disgraced for heading a French government that collaborated with Germany.

Nazis set up a military government in September 1943. Hitler also carved up Yugoslavia, absorbing much of Slovenia into the German Reich. The remaining parts of the country were put under direct German civil or military rule, or given to Hungary, Italy, Bulgaria, and Albania, to reward them for their support of the German war effort. Croatia remained a self-governing, collaborationist state.

Poland was also destroyed, reflecting Hitler's contempt for Polish lives and nationhood. Under the terms of the Nazi-Soviet Pact of 1939, Hitler and Soviet leader Joseph Stalin carved up the country between them. The Soviet Union occupied the eastern third of Poland until June 1941, when it came under attack from Germany. Hitler absorbed most of western Poland—renamed *Reichsgau Wartheland*—into the Third Reich. Central Poland became known as the General Government. It contained 12 million people, most of whom lived in the cities of Warsaw, Kraków, Radom, and Lublin. The General Government was presided over by Hans Frank. Frank was a German lawyer and politician. He directed a brutal program against Jews and other Poles, implementing Hitler's policies of mass extermination and slave labor.

Forced laborers

Millions of Poles were shipped off to labor camps, industrial plants, or farms in Germany. Most were worked to death over years of starvation and mistreatment. Hitler regarded the Slavic peoples, including the Poles and Russians, as "subhumans," whose only use was as a pool of cheap labor for Germany.

By 1944, the Germans had some seven million foreign nationals working as forced laborers, of whom 5,295,000 were civilians and 1,831,000 were prisoners of war. They accounted for 24 percent of the German workforce.

The Germans' treatment of forced laborers was often appalling. Workers often lived crammed together in basic, barn-like shelters in heavily guarded compounds. They were given meager rations of food, often no more than two bowls of thin soup and a piece of bread each day. Workers were subjected to daily physical abuse and many were shot on the spot, for little or no reason. Hundreds of thousands of people died of starvation or overwork.

Life for Polish Jews

Following the occupation of Poland in 1939, Hitler ordered the creation of ghettos to contain and control the country's Jews while he considered the broader question of how to remove Jews from the German Reich. German troops fenced or walled off sections of Polish towns and cities, into which they forced the country's Jews. The largest ghettos were in Warsaw, Lódz, Kraków, Lvov, and Lublin.

The conditions were ghastly. Severe overcrowding meant that typically seven people lived in a room. Many people were forced to survive on the streets. Sanitation was inadequate, and there were severe food shortages. On average, people received only 180 calories a day—less than 10 percent of the recommended daily intake. Bodies littered the streets, as hundreds of people died every day from disease and starvation. The only way out of the ghettos was death. In 1942, the Nazis implemented their "final solution" to the Jewish question. They began deporting Jews to extermination camps such as Auschwitz, Majdanek, Belzec, Treblinka, Chelmno, and Sobibor. There they were killed on a huge scale in what became known as the Holocaust.

Daily life in France

Elsewhere in Europe, particularly in France, the Low Countries, and

Members of the Danish Gestapo pose with their new weapons.

German soldiers salute officers who are mingling with Parisians at a café on the Champs Elysées.

WARSAW GHETTO UPRISING

The Warsaw Uprising was a landmark of bravery in the struggle against Nazi atrocities. Since occupying Poland in 1939, the Germans had forced hundreds of thousands of Polish Jews into the Warsaw ghetto. From July 1942, they began sending the Jews to an extermination camp at Treblinka. More than 300,000 had been deported by the beginning of October. A group of Jews in the ghetto organized the Jewish Fighting Organization (Zydowska Organizacja Bojowa, ZOB), led by Mordecai Anielewicz. They began small-scale resistance against the deportations in January 1943. On April 19, thousands of German troops supported by tanks moved into the ghetto to clear out its remaining inhabitants. Some 1,000 men from the ZOB and other resistance groups fought back with what small arms and explosives they had. The battle raged for almost a month before the resistance was crushed on May 16. Roughly 14,000 Jews were killed and 7,000 were deported.

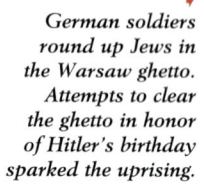

German soldiers round up Jews in the Warsaw ghetto. Attempts to clear the ghetto in honor of Hitler's birthday sparked the uprising.

Scandinavia, the German occupiers made some attempt at civility. Even in these areas, however, Nazi occupation meant regulation, deprivation, and suffering. In France, citizens had to adjust to a huge number of Nazi rules. Every civilian had to carry a thick wad of identity papers. They risked imprisonment if they failed to show the correct document on demand.

The papers included the *carte d'identité*, an identity card similar to a passport. Men of working age also had to carry a *fiche de démobilisation*. This card proved that they were not deserters or escaped prisoners of war. Later they had to show papers that exempted them from the German forced labor program, the *Service du Travail Obligatoire*.

The *carte d'alimentation*, or ration card, was the most significant official paper in the daily lives of French citizens. It entitled them to buy a small share of some basic foods; there was only just enough to survive on. The Nazis stripped France of its resources, leaving little for the French. German

Life in Occupied Europe

Eyewitness Report:

❝ I have seen nothing since the occupation of Greece by the Axis powers which could make me accept that this new order of things will be something just, moral, and humane. On the contrary, in everything that ... (they) have done, one sees injustice, immorality, and inhumanity, thieving, the plundering of every living thing by the invaders in order to make the population die of hunger, administrative injustice, terror, and police brutality daily. **❞**

Mario Rigouzzo, French consul on the island of Syros, Greece, February 1943

soldiers were given a worthless currency that enabled them to buy French goods very cheaply. Many German firms commandeered gasoline, leather, luxury goods, meat, and alcohol.

Almost all citizens used the black market—an illegal economy—to gain extra food. However, serious food shortages occurred during the winter months and got worse as the war went on. A typical main meal might consist of little more than a small piece of sausage, some green beans, a cube of cheese, and, for a few fortunate people, an egg.

Malnutrition and starvation

In Greece, the civilian population endured even greater hardship and suffering under German and Italian occupation, which began in April 1941.

Stocks of food, which were already low, were requisitioned to support the Axis war effort in North Africa. Within four months of occupying the country, the Germans had removed 14 million livestock from Greece and had forced farmers to hand over their crops. In addition, the British Royal Navy had blockaded the country, preventing the arrival of imported foods. British leaders said it was Germany's responsibility to feed the Greek population. They did not want to send supplies to the Greeks that the Germans could use for themselves. The result of the German and Allied actions was famine. During an unusually cold winter in 1941–42, an estimated 250,000 Greeks died of starvation and related diseases. Some 90 percent of babies died within days of being born.

Danish civilians wear traditional Jewish skull caps in the colors of the British RAF as a protest against their Nazi occupiers. The Nazis put a stop to this fashion in July 1943.

49

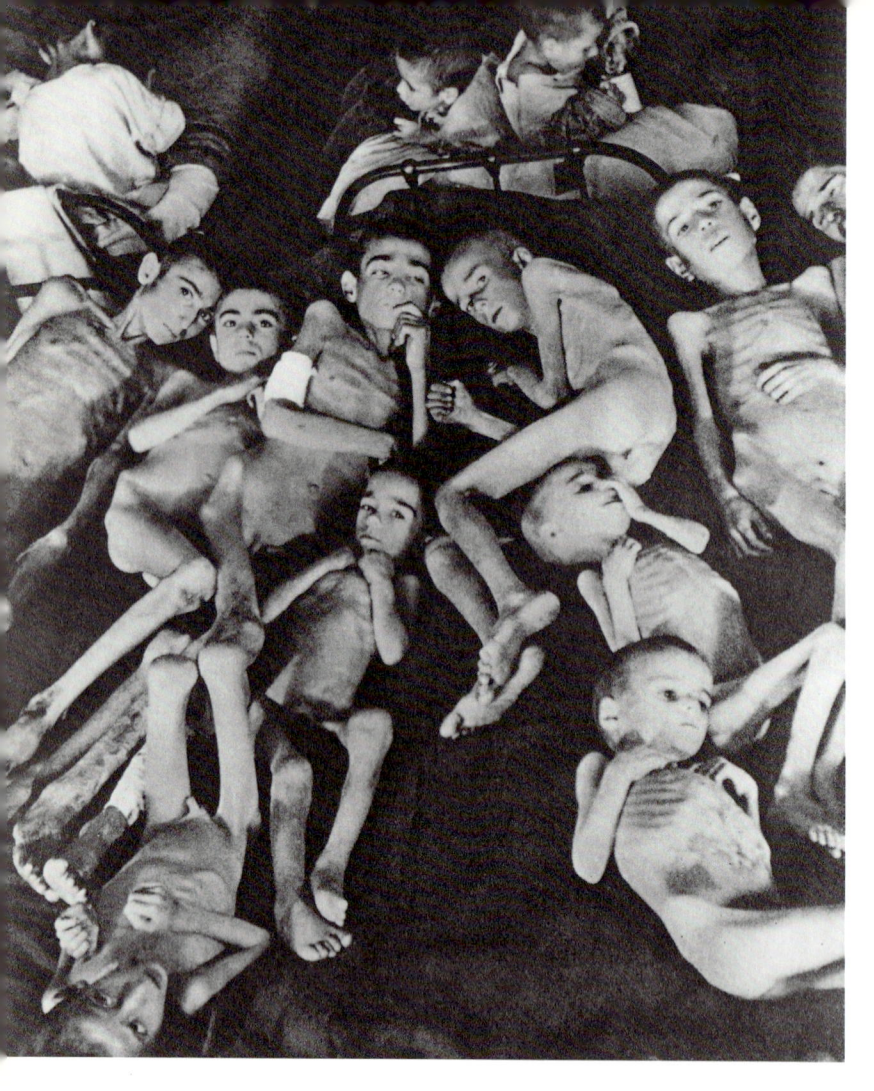

Malnourished children lie dying during the famine that struck Greece in the winter of 1941–42. The famine eased in spring 1942, when the Allies allowed the Red Cross to distribute relief supplies in the country.

Between fall 1944 and spring 1945, famine also struck Holland. After Dutch railroad workers went on strike to aid the Allied liberation of Europe, German forces retaliated by refusing to allow the distribution of food. Around 30,000 people starved to death as a result.

Seizure of property

While food was the most critical of the wartime shortages, occupation also affected many other areas of people's lives. Many civilians were forced to give up their homes to German officers and soldiers. In France, refugees who had been displaced by the German advance early in the war often returned to their houses to find entire German units living there.

In the Soviet Union, *Wehrmacht* (German Armed Forces) units took shelter from the harsh winter climate by expelling Russian peasant families from their simple homes. In some instances, the peasants froze to death within sight of their own homes. The seizure of property and displacement of people also occurred on a huge scale in Poland. German troops evicted hundreds of thousands of Poles in western Poland to make room for German settlers in the region.

Transportation became a huge problem as Germany requisitioned almost all available gasoline. In the Greek capital of Athens, a taxi became nothing more than a two-wheeled handcart pulled by a driver.

Shortages and curfews

In Paris the Germans issued only 7,000 driving permits to the city's entire civilian population. The restriction, combined with gasoline shortages, meant that some of Paris's busiest roads saw as few as 20 cars in an hour. Some inventive Parisians used automobiles powered by natural gas, which was held in tanks on the vehicles' roofs, or by steam.

The Germans also imposed curfews that required all citizens to be inside their homes at designated hours. Typical curfew hours ran from 10:00 PM to 5:30 AM, but sometimes they started as early as 5:00 PM hours. Anyone venturing on to the streets during the curfew was arrested. In eastern territories, in particular, they might be executed on the spot.

The list of deprivations suffered by the occupied peoples is long. Lack of soap contributed to poor hygiene and an increase in skin diseases. German coal requisitions deprived many people of heat during the winters. Prices of goods became inflated in the shops, further reducing what ordinary people could buy.

Life in Occupied Europe

These conditions, many of which were shared by citizens of the Allied nations, caused hardship for millions of people. Other aspects of German occupation, however, were more hated.

Persecution and death squads

The security forces that imposed Nazi rule were both feared and despised. *Einsatzgruppen*, or special action groups, operated on the Eastern Front. Their task was to follow the German advance and eliminate people the Nazis considered undesirable—mainly Jews, commissars (political leaders), and Roma (gypsies). The squads murdered some 15,000 people in Poland in 1939 alone. Many victims were made to dig their own graves before they were shot.

The *Einsatzgruppen* continued to conduct mass murder as the Germans moved into Soviet territory. In one notorious incident, they executed 34,000 Jews in late 1941 in the ravine of Babi Yar outside the Ukrainian capital, Kiev. Historians estimate that the *Einsatzgruppen* killed more than a million people on the Eastern Front, most of whom were Jews.

> "Prices of goods became inflated in the shops, further reducing what ordinary people could buy"

RESISTANCE

In every occupied country there were people who resisted German rule. Resistance was a huge drain on German manpower and resources. In occupied France, subversive underground newspapers such as *Combat* and *Franc-Tireur* were published. In addition, armed groups, including the Armée Secretè and the Maquis, carried out many actions, from killing German sentries to blowing up bridges. On the night before the Allied invasion of France in June 1944, members of the resistance blew up railroad lines, cut telephone wires, and laid thousands of mines to hamper the Germans.

After the German invasion of the Soviet Union in June 1941, communists became active in the resistance movement all over Europe. Their groups sometimes clashed with non-communist underground organizations. This happened in Yugoslavia, Poland, and Greece. Differences and conflicts between the groups lessened the potential strength of resistance.

Nonetheless, communist resistance movements played a huge part in weakening the German war effort. In the Soviet Union, around 150,000 partisans were operating from dense forests behind German lines by 1943. They controlled about 5,400 square miles (14,000 sq km) and killed around 35,000 German troops—although their actions also brought terrible reprisals upon civilians. In Yugoslavia, the communist Josip Broz, better known as Tito, headed a huge partisan army of about 200,000 men. Some 35 German divisions were tied down fighting the Yugoslav partisans, who also destroyed 18,000 German supply trains.

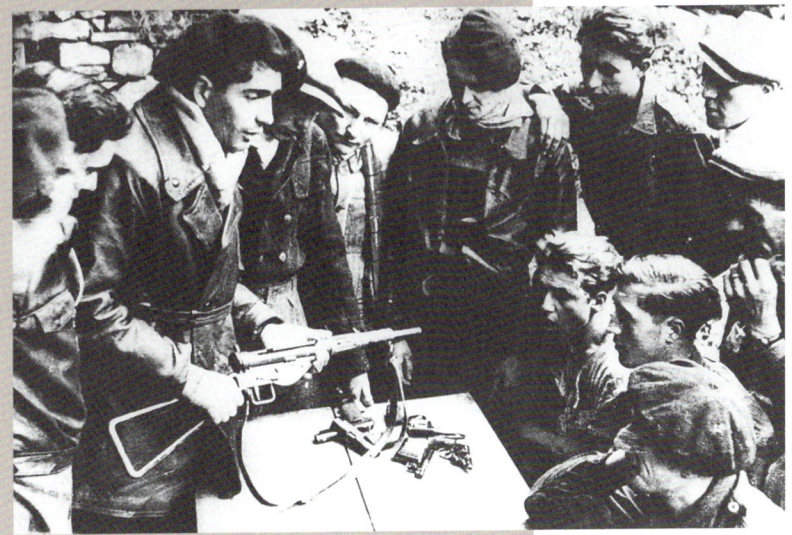

A resistance fighter from the French Maquis shows his compatriots how to strip a Sten gun.

The Home Fronts: Allied and Axis Life During World War II

PUNISHMENTS

The Germans responded to acts of resistance with terrible reprisals. One of the most notorious acts of reprisal followed the assassination by Czech resistance fighters of Reinhard Heydrich, the chief lieutenant of the Gestapo and governor of Bohemia and Moravia. After the killing, in June 1942, German troops targeted the Czech village of Lidice. They shot most of its male population—172 men—in the village square on June 10. They sent its women to their deaths in concentration camps, and dispersed the children throughout Germany to be brought up as Germans. They burned the village to the ground. Another massacre occurred in France on June 10, 1944, when German forces killed 642 men, women, and children in the town of Oradour-sur-Glane. This was in reprisal for resistance actions following the Allied invasion of France on June 6. In Yugoslavia, 5,000 men and young boys were executed during the night of October 20/21, 1941, near Kragujevac, after local partisans had fought the Germans.

Nazi soldiers watch as the village of Lidice burns. The Waffen-SS set the village on fire after massacring its male population.

A shortage of fuel has brought these streetcars in Germany to a standstill. By the end of the war, all parts of the German Reich were impoverished.

Life in Occupied Europe

A member of the Milice, France's paramilitary police, marches a group of arrested French citizens to their fate at Nazi hands. Under the Vichy regime, many French officials and civilians actively assisted the German war effort.

A member of the Einsatzgruppen murders a mother and child in eastern Europe.

Even in occupied territories free from such atrocities, citizens lived in constant fear of the Nazi police, which included various military police units. Most feared of all were the Nazis' political police units. They included the infamous *Geheime Staatspolizei* (Gestapo) and the *Sicherheitsdienst* (SD), the Reich's Security Service.

The Gestapo and SD hunted down "political" opponents within all the occupied territories. They seized people from the street or from their homes on very flimsy pretexts. Some people were denounced by neighbors with old grudges. Thousands of citizens disappeared, never to be seen again. On December 7, 1941, Hitler issued the so-called Night and Fog Decree. It instructed the military police that "persons endangering German security" should disappear into the "night and fog."

Living with the enemy

All over Europe many citizens resisted the German occupation, risking their lives to do so. The majority of the population could not resist openly. Countries such as Belgium and most of France were occupied for four years, and their citizens had to find a way of living alongside the occupiers. In Paris, the entertainers of the Moulin Rouge and Casino de Paris performed to large crowds that included many Nazi officers.

SPOTLIGHT

COLLABORATORS

In occupied Europe during World War II, there were many individuals who were later vilified as collaborators.

The entire populations of occupied countries had to work with the German authorities to a greater or lesser extent. However, there were individuals and groups that stepped across a line that was felt to be acceptable and were penalized for this. Sometimes the punishment was justified; sometimes not.

One level of collaboration was a personal one. Many women had relationships with German soldiers who were garrisoning their countries. In France in 1944, such women had their heads forcibly shaved and were paraded for everyone to see.

In France, collaboration was additionally complex because the Vichy government in southern France cooperated with the Germans until they took over late in 1942. Vichy officials helped transport Jews to the death camps, for example. After the war, Pierre Laval, the Prime Minister of Vichy France, was executed. The legacy of Vichy has left scars in the French political system that endure into the twenty-first century.

Some groups and individuals in occupied countries actually fought for the Germans. The *Waffen* ("Fighting") SS recruited troops from all of the nations occupied by Germany—even from those that the Nazi doctrine condemned as subhumans, such as Cossacks and Muslims from Bosnia. Sometimes this was because they could see advantages for themselves, and sometimes because they felt they had little alternative. This was particularly true in eastern Europe and the former Soviet Union, where collaboration with the Germans was seen as a way of escaping Stalin's tyranny.

Others were ideologically attracted to Nazi doctrines and enthusiastically embraced its tenets. The generic name for such collaborators comes from the name of the most famous of these sympathizers: "quisling," after Vidkun Quisling who set up a pro-German government in Norway.

Above: After the war came retribution against those who had collaborated with the Germans. These French women have had their heads shaved in public for having romantic relations with German soldiers, a relatively minor penalty given that, in some parts of Europe and the USSR, those suspected of collaborating with the Germans were executed without trial.

Above: Red Army general Andrei Vlasov (pictured here wearing glasses) was captured by the Germans in July 1942. He agreed to form a Russian Liberation Army, made up of anti-Stalinist Red Army prisoners of war. His force was not ready for action until 1944—many members of the Nazi hierarchy were virulently opposed to the idea. He surrendered to the Americans in Austria in 1945, but in May was captured by Soviet troops that surrounded the car in which he was traveling with a U.S. captain. He was taken to Moscow and hanged in August 1946.

Above: Pierre Laval, who served two terms as Prime Minister of Vichy France. He signed orders permitting the deportation of French Jews and of laborers sent to work in Germany. He later claimed that he had little choice and had tried to mitigate the effects of German demands, but he was clearly anti-Semitic. He was executed by firing squad in October 1945 after a controversial trial, most of which he refused to attend.

Right: Volunteers for the French Legion, a force raised to fight with the Germans in Russia, set off on the long journey east. Up to June 1941, the Nazi-Soviet Pact and the fact that Stalin forbade French communists from joining the Resistance against Hitler reinforced the dislike that many Frenchmen felt for the Soviet Union. Only after the start of Operation Barbarossa did French communists start organizing in Resistance groups. By 1944, they did their best to cover their inaction during the early years of occupation.

Life in Occupied Europe

Above: Belgian Leon Degrelle enthusiastically gives the Hitler salute. Degrelle had been a member of the right-wing Rexist party in pre-1939 Belgian politics. He joined the Walloon legion of the Wehrmacht in August 1941. The Walloons were transferred from the Wehrmacht to the control of the Waffen-SS in June 1943. Degrelle was badly wounded at Cherkassy in 1944. Early in 1945, he was made an SS-Obersturmbannführer (Lieutenant-Colonel) and was decorated with the Knight's Cross by Hitler himself. He escaped to Spain after the war, where he flagrantly proclaimed his sympathies with Nazism. He was condemned to death in his absence in Belgium, but died in Malaga in 1994.

Above left: Vidkun Quisling, the Norwegian who tried to impose his version of Nazism on Norway. Although the Germans did not fully trust him, he set up a party that recruited 35,000 members, and became "minister president." He was executed by firing squad in October 1945.

Above right: The Grand Mufti of Jerusalem meets Bosnian Muslim recruits to the Waffen-SS. A senior Muslim cleric, he was in charge of Jerusalem's Islamic holy places, but fled to Lebanon in 1937 because of his opposition to Zionism within the British Mandate of Palestine. He supported Nazi anti-Semitism and helped in recruiting Muslim volunteers. He died in Cairo in 1974.

Many French women also became romantically involved with German soldiers. They sometimes came to regret such relationships after the war, when their fellow citizens shamed and punished them as collaborators.

Joining the Nazis

A certain number of civilians in occupied countries actively supported the Nazi war effort, the persecution of Jews, or the suppression of their own countrymen. More than 300,000 male citizens and prisoners of war from France, Belgium, Holland, Norway, Denmark, Britain, Russia, and other countries joined the Waffen-SS and fought against the Allies.

In Poland, Lithuania, and Ukraine, a large proportion of the killing squads that executed Jews were local people. They often acted with the approval of the local church and political leaders. Many of the guards employed in Operation Reinhard—the murder of 2.3 million Polish Jews in the General Government—were Red Army prisoners of war, particularly Ukrainians. Anti-Semitism, or hatred of Jews, had a long history in some European countries. Nazi rule unleashed these prejudices. In Paris in August 1941, French anti-Semites destroyed Jewish shops and assaulted Jews throughout the city. The French police actively assisted the Germans in the roundup of French Jews for the concentration camps.

The days of occupation were times of survival, danger, and difficult moral choices for the people of Europe. Long-established ways of life and rules were swept aside, replaced with a fearsome and ruthlessly organized new regime. In such an uncertain world, many people conformed just to survive; others worked to resist Nazi rule.

TIMELINE
SEPTEMBER 1, 1939 – SEPTEMBER 2, 1945

SEPTEMBER 1
POLAND
A German force of 53 divisions, supported by 1,600 aircraft, crosses the German and Slovak borders into Poland in a pincer movement. World War II has begun.

SEPTEMBER 3
BRITAIN AND FRANCE
Britain and France declare war on Nazi Germany after the Nazis ignore their demands to immediately withdraw from Poland.

SEPTEMBER 9
POLAND
A Polish counterattack is launched over the Bzura River against Germany's Eighth Army. It only achieves short-term success. The Polish Army is rapidly falling to pieces under the relentless German attacks.

SEPTEMBER 17–30
POLAND
In accordance with a secret pact with Germany, the Soviet Red Army invades Poland. Little resistance is encountered on Poland's eastern border as the Polish Army is fighting for its life to the west.

SEPTEMBER 18–30
POLAND
Poland is defeated and split into two zones of occupation divided by the Bug River. Germany has lost 10,572 troops and the Soviet Union has 734 men killed in the campaign. Around 50,000 Poles are killed and 750,000 captured.

SEPTEMBER 29
SOVIET UNION
After occupying Poland, the Soviet Union concentrates on extending its control over the Baltic Sea region. During the next few weeks it gains bases and signs "mutual assistance" agreements with Lithuania, Latvia, and Estonia. Finland, however, will not agree to the Soviet Union's demands and prepares to fight.

OCTOBER 14
SEA WAR, NORTH SEA
The British battleship *Royal Oak* is sunk, with 786 lives lost, after *U-47* passes through antisubmarine defenses at Scapa Flow in the Orkneys.

NOVEMBER 30
EASTERN FRONT, FINLAND
A Soviet army of over 600,000 men, backed by air and naval power, attacks Finland. Highly-motivated Finnish troops use their familiarity with the terrain and use their ability to ski through snow-covered areas to launch hit-and-run raids on Red Army units bogged down in the snow.

DECEMBER 16
FINLAND
The Red Army begins a major new offensive. To compensate for their lack of armor and artillery, the Finns use improvised explosive devices ("Molotov Cocktails," named after the Soviet foreign minister) to destroy enemy tanks.

DECEMBER 13
ATLANTIC OCEAN
British ships fight the German pocket battleship *Graf Spee* at Battle of the River Plate. The *Graf Spee* is scuttled by its crew on the 17th.

1940

MARCH 11
FINLAND
The Treaty of Moscow between Finland and the Soviet Union is agreed, ending the Winter War. Finland retains its independence but has to surrender the Karelian Isthmus and Hangö – 10 percent of its territory. Campaign losses: 200,000 Soviet troops and 25,000 Finns.

APRIL 9
NORWAY/DENMARK
A German invasion force, including surface ships, U-boats, and 1,000 aircraft, attacks Denmark and Norway. Denmark is overrun immediately.

APRIL 14–19
NORWAY
An Allied expeditionary force of over 10,000 British, French, and Polish troops lands in Norway.

MAY 7–10
BRITAIN
Prime Minister Neville Chamberlain is severely criticized over the Norwegian campaign. He resigns and is replaced by Winston Churchill.

MAY 10
THE LOW COUNTRIES
German forces invade the Low Countries. But the main German attack will take place in the south, in the Ardennes region of France.

MAY 12–14
FRANCE
German forces reach the Meuse River and fight their way across at Sedan and Dinant on the 13th. German armor advances westward rapidly, opening a 50-mile (75-km) gap in the Allied line. Allied units retreat to the Channel port of Dunkirk.

MAY 26
FRANCE/BELGIUM
Operation Dynamo, the evacuation of Allied forces from the Dunkirk area, begins using small boats and naval vessels.

MAY 31
UNITED STATES
President Franklin D. Roosevelt launches a "billion-dollar defense program" to bolster the armed forces.

JUNE 1–9
NORWAY
After Britain and France reveal to the Norwegians that they are to begin an evacuation, troops begin to withdraw. King Haakon orders his Norwegians to stop fighting on June 9.

SEPTEMBER 1, 1939 – SEPTEMBER 2, 1945

June 3–4
FRANCE
Operation Dynamo ends. The remarkable operation has rescued 338,226 men—two-thirds of them British—from the Dunkirk beaches.

June 16–24
FRANCE
Marshal Henri-Philippe Pétain, the new French president, requests an armistice on the 17th. It is agreed on the 22nd. Germany occupies two-thirds of France, including the Channel and Atlantic coastlines.

July 1
ATLANTIC OCEAN
The "Happy Time" begins for U-boat crews as their range is increased now that they have bases in French ports. This lasts until October. U-boat crews inflict serious losses on Allied convoys.

July 10
BRITAIN
The Battle of Britain begins. Hermann Göring, the Nazi air force chief, orders attacks on shipping and ports in the English Channel.

July 21
SOVIET UNION
The Soviets annex Lithuania, Latvia, and Estonia.

August 24–25
BRITAIN
The Luftwaffe inflicts serious losses on the Royal Air Force (RAF) during attacks on its main air bases in southeast England, straining the resources of Fighter Command to breaking point in a few days.

August 26–29
GERMANY
The RAF launches a night raid with 81 aircraft on Berlin following a similar raid on London. Hitler is outraged and vows revenge. German aircraft are redirected to make retaliatory raids on London. This relieves the pressure on Fighter Command's air bases.

September 7–30
AIR WAR, BRITAIN
Full-scale bombing raids on London—the "Blitz"—begin with 500 bombers and 600 fighters.

October 28
GREECE
Italy attacks Greece from Albania. The winter weather limits air support and thousands die of cold.

November 5
UNITED STATES
President Franklin D. Roosevelt is elected for a third term.

November 11–12
MEDITERRANEAN
At the Battle of Taranto, British torpedo aircraft from the carrier *Illustrious* destroy three Italian battleships and damage two other vessels during the raid on the Italian base.

December 9–11
EGYPT
The British launch their first offensive in the Western Desert. The Western Desert Force (31,000) attacks the fortified camps that have been established by the Italians in Egypt. Some 34,000 Italians are taken prisoner as they retreat rapidly from Egypt.

1941

January 2
POLITICS, UNITED STATES
President Franklin D. Roosevelt announces a program to produce 200 freighters—"Liberty" ships—to support the Allied Atlantic convoys.

February 14
NORTH AFRICA
To aid the faltering Italians, the first units of General Erwin Rommel's Afrika Korps land at Tripoli.

March 11
UNITED STATES
President Franklin D. Roosevelt signs the Lend-Lease Act that allows Britain to obtain supplies without having to immediately pay for them in cash.

April 6–15
YUGOSLAVIA/GREECE
Thirty-three German divisions, with Italian and Hungarian support, invade Yugoslavia from the north, east, and southeast. German forces also attack Greece from the north.

April 17
YUGOSLAVIA
Yugoslavia surrenders to Germany. Immediately, guerrilla forces emerge to resist the Nazi occupation.

April 27
GREECE
German forces occupy Athens. Campaign dead: Greek 15,700; Italian 13,755; German 1,518; and British 900.

May 20–22
CRETE
A German force of 23,000 men, supported by 600 aircraft, attacks Crete. The Germans launch the first major airborne operation in history.

May 23–27
ATLANTIC OCEAN
British ships find the German battleship *Bismarck* and cruiser *Prinz Eugen* in the Denmark Straits between Iceland and Greenland. The *Bismarck* sinks the cruiser *Hood* and damages the battleship *Prince of Wales*, but is then sunk.

May 28–31
CRETE
Crete falls to the Germans. British losses are 1,742 men, plus 2,011 dead and wounded at sea, while Germany has 3,985 men killed.

June 22
SOVIET UNION
Germany launches Operation Barbarossa, the invasion of the Soviet Union, with three million men divided into three army groups along a 2000-mile (3200-km) front. Army Group North strikes toward the Baltic and Leningrad. Army Group Center aims to take Smolensk and then Moscow. Army Group South advances toward the Ukraine and the Caucasus.

July 31
GERMANY
Reinhard Heydrich, Germany's security chief and head of the SS secret police, receives orders to begin creating a draft plan for the murder of the Jews, which becomes known as the "Final Solution."

September 30
SOVIET UNION
Operation Typhoon, the German attack on Moscow, officially begins.

TIMELINE

November 26
PACIFIC OCEAN
The Japanese First Air Fleet leaves the Kurile Islands on a mission to destroy the U.S. Pacific Fleet at Pearl Harbor, Hawaii.

December 7
HAWAII
The Japanese attack Pearl Harbor. Over 183 Japanese aircraft destroy six battleships and 188 aircraft, damage or sink 10 other vessels, and kill 2,000 servicemen. The Japanese lose 29 aircraft.

December 8
SOVIET UNION
Adolf Hitler reluctantly agrees to suspend the advance on Moscow for the duration of the winter.

December 11
AXIS
Germany and Italy declare war on the United States.

1942

January 10–11
DUTCH EAST INDIES
A Japanese force begins attacking the Dutch East Indies to secure the oil assets of this island-chain.

January 20
GERMANY
At the Wannsee Conference, Berlin, deputy head of the SS Reinhard Heydrich reveals his plans for the "Final Solution" to the so-called "Jewish problem." Heydrich receives permission to begin deporting all Jews in German-controlled areas to Eastern Europe to face either forced labor or extermination.

February 8–14
SINGAPORE
Japanese troops capture Singapore. Japan has fewer than 10,000 casualties in Malaya. British forces have lost 138,000 men.

April 9
PHILIPPINES
Major General Jonathan Wainright, commanding the U.S. and Filipino forces, surrenders to the Japanese.

April 18
JAPAN
Lieutenant Colonel James Doolittle leads 16 B-25 bombers, launched from the carrier *Hornet*, against targets in Japan, including Tokyo.

June 4
PACIFIC OCEAN
The Battle of Midway begins. Japan's Admiral Chuichi Nagumo aims to seize the U.S. base at Midway and then destroy the U.S. Pacific Fleet. Japan deploys 165 vessels, including eight carriers. The U.S. Navy has a smaller force but has three carriers. The loss of half of its carrier strength in the battle, plus 275 aircraft, puts Japan on the defensive in the Pacific.

June 21
LIBYA
Following the Allied withdrawal into Egypt, the Tobruk garrison falls following German land and air attacks.

June 28
SOVIET UNION
Germany launches its summer offensive, Operation Blue, with its Army Group South attacking east from Kursk toward Voronezh.

July 4–10
SOVIET UNION
The siege of Sevastopol ends with the Germans capturing 90,000 men.

August 7–21
GUADALCANAL
The U.S. 1st Marine Division lands on Guadalcanal Island to overwhelm the Japanese garrison.

September 2
POLAND
The Nazis are "clearing" the Jewish Warsaw Ghetto. Over 50,000 Jews have been killed by poison gas or sent to concentration camps.

October 23
EGYPT
The Battle of El Alamein begins. An attack by 195,000 Allied troops against 104,000 Axis men begins.

November 2–24
EGYPT/LIBYA
Rommel, severely lacking supplies, decides to withdraw from El Alamein. Germany and Italy have lost 59,000 men killed, wounded, or captured. The Allies have suffered 13,000 killed, wounded, or missing.

November 19
SOVIET UNION
General Zhukov launches a Soviet counteroffensive at Stalingrad to trap the Germans in a massive pincer movement.

1943

February 2
SOVIET UNION
The siege of Stalingrad ends. Field Marshal Friedrich Paulus and 93,000 German troops surrender.

February 14–22
TUNISIA
In the Battle of Kasserine Pass, Rommel's forces cause panic among U.S. troops. He loses 2,000 men; the Americans 10,000.

April 17
GERMANY
The U.S. Eighth Army Air Force attacks Bremen's aircraft factories from its bases in eastern England. Sixteen of the 115 B-17 Flying Fortress bombers from the raid are lost.

May 13
TUNISIA
Axis forces surrender. Some 620,000 casualties and prisoners have been sustained by Germany and Italy. Allied campaign losses: French 20,000; British 19,000; and U.S. 18,500.

July 5
SOVIET UNION
Over 6000 German and Soviet tanks and assault guns take part in the Battle of Kursk.

July 9
SICILY
U.S. and British troops begin the attack on Sicily.

July 12–13
SOVIET UNION
At Kursk, the Soviets launch a counteroffensive around Prokhorovka and an enormous tank battle develops. The German offensive is defeated.

SEPTEMBER 1, 1939 – SEPTEMBER 2, 1945

AUGUST 11–17
SICILY
The Germans finally start withdrawing before U.S. forces enter Messina on the 17th.

SEPTEMBER 9
ITALY
Lieutenant General Mark Clark's U.S. Fifth Army, plus the British X Corps, lands in the Gulf of Salerno.

SEPTEMBER 25
SOVIET UNION
The Soviets recapture Smolensk in their continuing offensive. Germany's Army Group Center is now falling back in some disarray.

NOVEMBER 6
SOVIET UNION
The Soviets recapture Kiev.

DECEMBER 26
ARCTIC OCEAN
At the Battle of the North Cape, the German battleship *Scharnhorst* is sunk.

1944

JANUARY 14–27
SOVIET UNION
The Red Army ends the German blockade of Leningrad. Some 830,000 civilians have died during the siege.

JANUARY 22
ITALY
Troops of the Allied VI Corps make an amphibious landing at Anzio, behind the German lines.

MARCH 7–8
BURMA/INDIA
Operation U-Go, the Japanese offensive to drive the Allies back into India by destroying their bases at Imphal and Kohima, begins.

MARCH 20–22
ITALY
Despite further frontal attacks by New Zealand troops, the German defenders repulse all efforts to dislodge them from Monte Cassino.

MAY 18
ITALY
The Allies capture the monastery of Monte Cassino.

JUNE 6
FRANCE
The Allies launch the greatest amphibious operation in military history—D-Day. Some 50,000 men land on five invasion beaches to establish a toehold in Normandy. Allied casualties are 2,500 dead.

JUNE 19–21
PHILIPPINE SEA
Battle of the Philippine Sea. Japan's Combined Fleet is defeated by the U.S. Fifth Fleet. The Japanese lose 346 aircraft and two carriers. U.S. losses are 30 aircraft and slight damage to a battleship.

JUNE 22
SOVIET UNION
The Red Army launches Operation Bagration against Germany's Army Group Center.

JULY 20
GERMANY
An attempt is made by German officers to assassinate Adolf Hitler. It fails to kill the Führer.

AUGUST 1
POLAND
The Warsaw uprising begins. Some 38,000 soldiers of the Polish Home Army battle with about the same number of German troops.

AUGUST 25
FRANCE
The commander of the German garrison of Paris, General Dietrich von Choltitz, surrenders to the Allies.

SEPTEMBER 17
HOLLAND
Operation Market Garden, an Allied armored and airborne thrust across Holland to outflank the German defenses, begins. Paratroopers land at Arnhem, Eindhoven, and Nijmegen to capture vital bridges.

SEPTEMBER 22–25
HOLLAND
The paratroopers fall back from Arnhem, leaving 2,500 dead behind.

OCTOBER 2
POLAND
The last Poles in Warsaw surrender as the Germans crush the uprising. Polish deaths number 150,000. The Germans have lost 26,000 men.

OCTOBER 20
PHILIPPINES
As the U.S. Sixth Army lands on Leyte Island, General Douglas MacArthur wades ashore and keeps a promise he made two years earlier: "I shall return."

OCTOBER 23–26
PHILIPPINES
Following the U.S. landings on Leyte, the Japanese Combined Fleet is defeated at the Battle of Leyte Gulf.

DECEMBER 16–22
BELGIUM
Hitler launches Operation Watch on the Rhine, his attempt to capture Antwerp. The thick fog means the Germans achieve complete surprise. But they fail to capture Bastogne.

1945

JANUARY 9
PHILIPPINES
The U.S. Sixth Army makes unopposed amphibious landings on Luzon.

JANUARY 27
POLAND
The Red Army liberates the Nazi death camp at Auschwitz.

JANUARY 28
BELGIUM
The last bits of the German "bulge" in the Ardennes are wiped out. The Germans have lost 100,000 killed, wounded, and captured in their defeat. The Americans have lost 81,000 killed, wounded, or captured, and the British 1,400 killed.

JANUARY 30
GERMANY
The Red Army is only 100 miles (160 km) from Berlin.

FEBRUARY 4–11
SOVIET UNION
Marshal Joseph Stalin, President Franklin D. Roosevelt, and Prime Minister Winston Churchill meet at the Yalta Conference in the Crimea to discuss postwar Europe. The "Big Three" decide that Germany will be divided into four zones, administered

TIMELINE

by Britain, France, the United States, and the Soviet Union.

FEBRUARY 13–14
GERMANY
The RAF mounts a night raid on Dresden. The 805 bombers inflict massive damage on the city, killing 50,000 people.

FEBRUARY 17
IWO JIMA
Under the command of Lieutenant General Holland M. Smith, the U.S. Marines land on the island of Iwo Jima. The attackers are hit by intense artillery and small-arms fire from the 21,000-man Japanese garrison.

MARCH 16
IWO JIMA
The island of Iwo Jima is declared secure by the Americanst. They have lost 6,821 soldiers and sailors dead, while of the 21,000 Japanese garrison, only 1,083 are taken prisoner.

MARCH 22–31
GERMANY
The Allied crossings of the Rhine River begin. German resistance is negligible.

APRIL 1
OKINAWA
Operation Iceberg, the U.S. invasion of the island, commences. The island, only 325 miles (520 km) from Japan, has two airfields on the western side and two partially-protected bays on the east coast—an excellent springboard for the proposed invasion of the Japanese mainland.

APRIL 7
PACIFIC OCEAN
The Japanese *Yamato*, the world's largest battleship, is sunk at sea during an attack by U.S. warplanes.

APRIL 9
ITALY
The final campaign in Italy begins as the U.S. Fifth and British Eighth Armies attack the Germans.

APRIL 12
UNITED STATES
President Franklin D. Roosevelt dies of a cerebral haemorrhage. Vice President Harry S. Truman takes over the position of president.

APRIL 16
GERMANY
The Soviet offensive to capture Berlin commences with a total of 2.5 million men, 41,600 guns and mortars, 6,250 tanks and self-propelled guns, and 7,500 combat aircraft. The Germans have one million men, 10,400 guns and mortars, 1,500 tanks or assault guns, and 3,300 combat aircraft.

APRIL 27
GERMANY
"Fortress Berlin" has been reduced to an east-to-west belt 10 miles (16 km) long by three miles (5 km) wide. German forces within the city are affected by widespread desertions and suicides.

APRIL 28
ITALY
Former Italian dictator Benitto Mussolini and his mistress Claretta Petacci are captured by partisans. They are both shot.

APRIL 30
GERMANY
Adolf Hitler and Eva Braun commit suicide in the Führerbunker in Berlin.

MAY 2
GERMANY
Following a savage three-day battle, in which half the garrison has been killed, Berlin, the capital of Nazi Germany, falls to the Red Army.

MAY 3
BURMA
Following 38 months of Japanese occupation, Rangoon falls to the Allies without a fight.

JUNE 22
OKINAWA
All Japanese resistance on the island ends. The Japanese have lost 110,00 killed during the fighting. The U.S. Tenth Army has suffered 7,613 men killed or missing, and 31,807 wounded.

JULY 17–AUGUST 2
GERMANY
The Potsdam Conference takes place in Berlin. The "Big Three"—U.S. President Harry Truman, Soviet leader Marshal Joseph Stalin, and British Prime Minister Clement Attlee (who had defeated Churchill in a general election on July 5)—meet to discuss postwar policy. Japan is informed that an immediate surrender would result in the continued existence of its nation, but further resistance will lead to the "utter devastation of the Japanese homeland." This is a veiled reference to the use of atomic weapons against Japan itself.

AUGUST 6
JAPAN
The B-29 Superfortress *Enola Gay* drops an atomic bomb on the Japanese city of Hiroshima, killing 70,000 people and wounding 100,000.

AUGUST 9
MANCHURIA
A massive Soviet offensive by 1.5 million men begins against the Japanese Kwantung Army.

AUGUST 9
JAPAN
A second U.S. atomic bomb is dropped on Nagasaki. It kills 35,000 people and injures a further 60,000.

AUGUST 10
JAPAN
Following a conference, during which the emperor voices his support for an immediate acceptance of the Potsdam Proclamation, Japan announces its willingness to surrender unconditionally.

AUGUST 23
MANCHURIA
The campaign in Manchuria ends in total Soviet victory. The Japanese have lost over 80,000 dead and 594,000 taken prisoner. Soviet losses are 8,000 men killed and 22,000 wounded. The Kwantung Army has been destroyed.

SEPTEMBER 2
ALLIES
Aboard the battleship *Missouri* in Tokyo Bay, Japanese officials sign the Instrument of Surrender, bringing World War II to a close.

GLOSSARY

assassination A murder carried out for a political reason.

Axis One of the two groups of combatants in the war. The leading Axis powers were Germany, Italy, and Japan.

black market An illegal trade in goods that is against official regulations.

blackout A requirement that no lights can be visible during darkness in order not to illuminate targets or routes for the enemy.

censorship Controlling the information that people are allowed to communicate, often to protect military secrecy.

civil defense Measures to protect the civilian population during wartime, such as protection against air raids.

collaborator Someone who works with occupation authorities or who helps their cause.

curfew A regulation that people may not be outside between certain hours, usually at night.

draft The compulsory enlistment of people into the armed forces.

evacuee Someone who has been moved from his or her home to a safer place for protection from enemy attacks.

gas mask A mask that fits tightly over the face to protect the wearer from poisonous gas.

ghetto An enclosed part of a city in which Jews were forced to live.

Holocaust The systematic German campaign to exterminate millions of Jews and others.

internment Confining enemy citizens in camps.

morale The spirit of a people and how optimistic or pessimistic they feel about success or failure.

Nazi A member of Adolf Hitler's National Socialist German Workers' Party.

neutral A country that does not take sides in order to remain outside a conflict.

newsreel A short movie that reports on current events.

occupation The seizure and control of an area by military force.

partisans Guerrillas who operate behind enemy lines.

patriotism A love for one's country.

propaganda Information that is presented in a biased way to make people either support one particular view or be hostile toward another.

rationing A system of limiting food and other supplies to ensure that everyone gets a similar amount.

reprisals Punishments that are carried out in retaliation for a specific action.

requisition To seize civilian possessions for military use.

resistance A secret organization in a conquered country that organizes attacks and sabotage against the occupying forces.

sabotage To destroy infrastructure, such as railroads or factories, in order to damage a country's war effort.

war bonds Savings certificates that governments sold to their populations to raise money to finance the conflict.

FURTHER READING

»»»» BOOKS

Adams, Simon. *Under Occupation* (World War II). North Mankato, MN: Sea to Sea Books, 2009.

Adams, Simon. *Occupation and Resistance* (Documenting World War II). New York, NY: Rosen Central, 2008.

Burgan, Michael. *Refusing to Crumble: The Danish Resistance in World War II* (Taking a Stand). North Mankato, MN: Compass Point Books, 2010.

Cooke, Alistair. *Alistair Cooke's American Journey: Life on the Home Front in the Second World War.* New York, NY: Penguin Books, 2007.

Cooke, Alistair. *The American Home Front: 1941–1942.* New York, NY: Grove Press, 2007.

Gardiner, Juliet. *War on the Home Front: Experience Life in Britain During the Second World War.* London, England: Carlton Publishing Group, 2012.

Gitlin, Martin. *World War II on the Home Front: An Interactive History Adventure* (You Choose Books). North Mankato, MN: Capstone Press, 2012.

Hazen, Walter. *World War II: Everyday Life.* Culver City, CA: Good Year Books, 2006.

Kent, Deborah. *The Tragic History of the Japanese–American Internment Camps* (From Many Cultures, One History). Berkeley Heights, NJ: Enslow Publishers, 2008.

Macdonald, Fiona. *World War II: Life on the Home Front: A Primary Source History* (In Their Own Words). New York, NY: Gareth Stevens Publishing, 2009.

Michael O'Mara Books Ltd. *Eating for Victory: Healthy Home Front Cooking on War Rations: Reproductions of Official Second World War Instruction Leaflets.* London, England: Michael O'Mara Books, 2007.

Michael O'Mara Books Ltd. *Make Do and Mend: Keeping Family and Home Afloat on War Rations: Reproductions of Official Second World War Instruction Leaflets.* London, England: Michael O'Mara Books, 2007.

Millgate, Helen D. (ed.). *Mr. Brown's War: A Diary from the Home Front.* Stroud, England: The History Press, 2011.

Samuels, Charlie. *Life Under Occupation* (World War II Sourcebook). London, England: Brown Bear Books, 2012.

»»»» WEB SITES

Due to the changing nature of Internet links, Rosen Publishing had developed an online list of websites related to this subject. This site is updated regularly. Please use this link to access the list:

http://www.rosenlinks.com/WW2/Home

INDEX

A

Anderson, John 18
Anderson Shelter 18
Anzio 59
Arcadia Conference 6
Ardennes 59
Army Air Force Band 9
Arnhem 59
Attlee, Clement 60
Autry, Gene 9

B

B-17 Flying Fortress 8
Babi Yar 51
Badoglio, Pietro 37
Barbarossa, Operation 57
Berlin 60
Bevan, Ernest 22
Bismarck 57
Boy Scouts 10
Braun, Eva 60
Britain, Battle of 57

C

Chamberlain, Neville 18, 56
Chechens 27
Chrysler 9
Churchill, Winston 22, 56, 59

D

Degrelle, Leon 55
DiMaggio, Joe 9
Douglas, Melvyn 7
Dresden 35, 60
Dunkirk 56
Dynamo, Operation 56, 57

E

Einsatzgruppen 51, 53
El Alamein, Battle of 58
Enola Gay 60
Executive Order 9066 10, 14

F

Fairbanks, Douglas 9
Feller, Bob 9
Fonda, Henry 9
Ford 9
Frank, Hans 46

G

Gable, Clark 9
General Motors 9
Gestapo 53
Goebbels, Joseph 32, 34
Graf Spee 56
Great Depression 8, 15, 23
Greater Japan Women's Association 40
Greater Japan Youth Corps 40, 41
gulag 24

H

Hamburg 35
Heydrich, Reinhard 52, 58
Hiroshima 60
Hitler, Adolf 19, 30, 35, 44, 45, 46, 47, 55, 58, 59, 60
Hitler Youth 32, 34
Hollywood 12
Home Guard 22
HMS *Hood* 57

I

Imperial Rule Assistance Association 40
Industrial Patriotic League 40
Ingushetians 27
Iwo Jima 60

K

Kaiser, Henry 9
Kasserine Pass, Battle of 58
Kreisau Circle 36
Kursk, Battle of 58

L

LaGuardia, Fiorello 7
Laval, Pierre 54
Lend-Lease Act 57
Leningrad 27
Leyte Gulf, Battle of 59
Lidice 52
Local Defense Volunteers 22
Luftwaffe 19, 24, 34, 57

M

Maquis 51
Market Garden, Operation 59

INDEX

Midway, Battle of 40, 58
Milice 53
Military Powers Act 20
Miller, Glenn 9
Monte Cassino 59
Morrison, Herbert 18
Morrison Shelter 18
Moscow 24, 30
Mussolini, Benito 35, 37, 60

N

Nagasaki 60
Naples 38
National Association for the Advancement of Colored People 13
Night and Fog Decree 53
NKVD 26
North Africa 30, 36, 49
North Cape, Battle of 59

O

Office of Civilian Defense 7
Office of Price Administration 7
Okinawa 15, 60
Oradour-sur-Glane 52

P

Pearl Harbor 6, 10, 39, 58
People's Volunteer Units 40
Pétain, Henri-Philippe 45, 46, 57
Philippine Sea, Battle of 59
Phoney War 19

Pius XII, Pope
Potsdam Conference 60
HMS *Prince of Wales* 57
Probst, Christoph 36
Pyle, Ernie 15

Q

Quisling, Vidkun 45, 54, 55

R

Reagan, Ronald 9
Red Orchestra 36
Rome 38
Rommel, Erwin 57
Roosevelt, Eleanor 7
Roosevelt, Franklin D. 6, 8, 10, 56, 57, 59, 60
Rosie the Riveter 10, 11
Royal Air Force 57
Russian Liberation Army 54

S

Sauckel, Fritz 31
Scholl, Hans 36
Scholl, Sophie 36
Schutzstaffel 57
Speer, Albert 35
Spitfire 21
Stalin, Joseph 24, 25, 26, 46, 54, 59, 60
Stalingrad 58
Stewart, James 9

T

Taranto, Battle of 57
Tarawa 13

Terboven, Josef 45
Third Reich 31, 46
Treaty of Moscow 56
Truman, Harry 60
Turin 35, 36, 37
Turkel, Studs 14
Typhoon, Operation 57

U

U-boats 6, 19
Uhrig-Römer Group 36
Ural Mountains 26

V

Vlasov, Andrei 54

W

Waffen-SS 52, 55
Wansee Conference 58
Warsaw Ghetto 58
Wehrmacht 50
Western Desert Force 57
White Rose group 36
Williams, Ted 9
Winter War 56
Women Accepted for Volunteer Emergency Service 10
Women's Army Auxiliary Corps 10
Women's Land Army 20

Y

Yalta Conference 59